Parallel Lives

(Conversations with Luis)

Eddie Rooney

Published by New Generation Publishing in 2021

First Edition

ISBN: 978-1-80031-116-9

www.newgeneration-publishing.com

New Generation Publishing

*In memory of Denis Scullion and Peter Sullivan -
¡mejores no hay !*

Either character or circumstance may be the basis of a "sunkrisis" (comparison); similar events affecting dissimilar persons and similar persons reacting to contrasting events alike provide a suitable field for the exercise. It is basically a rhetorical procedure; but it is rescued from purely rhetorical ingenuity by its value as a way of concentrating and directing the moral reflections which are the primary purpose of biography.

D.A. Russell, Plutarch (London, 1973)

Table of Contents

Introduction

No man ever steps in the same river twice, for it's not the same river and he's not the same man.

Heraclitus

Looking back, the shared concerns about the dire consequences of divisions between peoples which are discussed in the following pages should have become apparent even at the first fortuitous meeting in a bar-restaurant in Mallorca which brought together two perfect strangers. One, a Scottish visitor to the Island, regarded by some of his family and friends as a bit of a dreamer whose unremarkable, apparently unambitious, and to the casual onlooker rather boring life, saw him teach for thirty years in the same High school in Coatbridge, a small town of approximately 44,000 inhabitants located mid-way between Scotland's two major cities – Glasgow and the Capital, Edinburgh. The other, Mallorquín born and bred, was a former Jesuit priest whose laicization allowed him to concentrate on what he came increasingly to consider his more demanding and rewarding work with UNESCO which entailed meetings and missions in many of the world's hotspots.

The idea for the following account of my gradual emergence from the relative comfort of my background, and of the events and people who have contributed to making that life-changing educational journey possible, came to me during one of the many conversations I have had with that Spanish friend whom I met many years ago. I was interested in combining that idea with an account of my friend's very different background and life experience and of the events and situations in our lives which have shaped our views on historical differences between people which continue to create major problems in societies. Fortunately, he was very open to the idea and gave me all the encouragement I needed.

The change in my view of the world, and indeed the fact that there even was a world out there which mattered, was gradual. In my ignorance I was blissfully unaware of just how little I knew about other countries or cultures.

"People rarely appreciate their ignorance because they lock themselves inside an echo chamber of like-minded friends and self-confirming news feeds, where their beliefs are constantly reinforced and seldom challenged."[1]

I began to challenge my own view of the world when, in my teenage years, I started to holiday abroad - the first of my family to be able to do so. Those first forays outside my east-end of Glasgow working class comfort zone introduced me to a different world and aroused in me a curiosity about other countries and cultures which has continued to this day. In a conscious effort to broaden my horizons I immersed myself in the literature of the countries I had visited and the ones I hoped to visit but so far never have. The more I experienced on my travels, and the more I realised how little I knew about life, I was forced increasingly to give serious thought to the seemingly insoluble problem of how to overcome apparently irreconcilable differences between peoples. As a result, I became convinced of the responsibility we all of us have, as members of the human race, to seek ways to accommodate differences – of class, race, and political

---

[1] Yuval Noah Harari: 21 Lessons for the 21st Century, p255

or religious beliefs in particular – in order to ensure peaceful co-existence between and within nations, communities and individuals. For too many people from my background in the West of Scotland, for example, there was, and indeed there still is, unfortunately, no meeting point between some so-called followers of different branches of Christianity. Of course, many of the religious differences in Scotland derive from historical events in Ireland, more of which later.

History is littered with examples of the disastrous and more often than not bloody, if not genocidal, consequences of attempts – successful or otherwise – to impose a set of beliefs or an alien way of life on others, frequently in the guise of introducing the recipients to the benefits of 'civilisation', 'true religion' or a particular 'political system.' Given the horrific violence, enslavement, loss of culture and language and terrible injustices visited upon indigenous populations by rapacious colonisers one cannot fail to challenge the idea that any so-called civilising benefits could justify what, in some cases, amounted to near genocide. One only has to think of the Crusades, fought over the Holy Land in the 11th, 12th and 13th centuries, the near extermination of indigenous tribes in North, Central and South America by European colonists, the treatment of the aborigines in Australia, Stalin's Great Purge which resulted in just under a million 'legal' deaths and many, many more in the Gulags, the Cambodian Killing Fields where more than a million people were killed and buried by the Khmer Rouge regime during its rule of the country in the late 1970s, the horrors of the Holocaust which resulted in the murder of more than six million Jews, the genocide in Rwanda, the Islamic State's war on "infidels" and the "shock and awe" which the so-called Pax Americana visited on the people of Iraq. These are but a few historical examples of campaigns carried out with the specific aim of acquiring new territories for the expansion of political, religious or economic interest.

Historical events such as these have frequently, if not inevitably, resulted in bitterness and conflict, often after years of simmering anger, resentment and frustration over failure to address obvious injustices. It goes without saying, of course, that I do not have, nor could I possibly have, personal experience of all the injustices suffered by people throughout history and therefore cannot possibly express the views of those whose lives have been affected by such injustices. For that reason, the following pages draw solely on the experiences in Spain, Portugal, Chile, Sarajevo, Kosovo, Ireland and Scotland, of two old friends who, despite their totally different social, educational and experiential backgrounds, have had to confront the often bitter consequences of an *Us and Them* mentality.

From the outset, in my conversations with Luis Ignacio Ramallo Massanet, there was a mutual recognition of the need to encourage dialogue between antagonistic factions with entrenched, opposing views, while at the same time recognising the great difficulty of promoting understanding of the *Other's* way of life. While it is incumbent on all of us to do what is in our power to combat the negative effects of race, class, political or religious differences, in order to do so it is important to challenge, and call out, those populists who appeal to raw emotions as their way of fostering hate and division for personal, political or economic self-interest.

Originality of subject matter in works of literature are rare – although perhaps not so rare as the one or two per century suggested by Pierre Boulle in his novel *La Planète des Singes* – and so most writers inevitably deal with subjects which have already been covered in some form or another by previous authors. The themes considered in the present work are no different and I readily acknowledge the influence those authors listed in *the Bibliography* have had on my approach to the task of recounting the experiences of two old friends.

Chapter 1

Tempus Fugit

*My contemplations are of Time
That has transfigured me*
W.B.Yeats

An early morning phone call a few days into a long-anticipated holiday brought the devastating news of the sudden and untimely death of one of my closest and dearest friends. The passing of Denis Scullion, a colleague and confidant for almost forty years and my constant walking companion on the Camino de Santiago - the medieval pilgrim route through France and Spain – was a cruel reminder of how tenuously we cling to life.

Having long since passed the biblical three score years and ten and having given little thought to my own mortality, I was abruptly confronted with the harshest of life's realities. Unpretentious, always there when needed, always considerate of others and a constant source of strength, support and honesty, Denis, one of life's good guys, one of those who restore one's faith in humanity, had gone before me and I was left to mourn his passing and to face up to, and come to terms with, my own rapidly advancing years.

Since completing my second book, *Old Ambrosians on the Chemin de Saint Jacques,* in which I recount the many experiences I had during my travels on the Way of St James with Denis and Tom Milligan, another good friend and colleague, I had found it extremely difficult to take up the pen again, although there were some recurring themes and past events which I felt compelled to commit to paper before increasing memory lapses made it impossible to do so. Of course, it is impossible to write about past events, and people who have influenced one's social and educational development, without making reference to past circumstances and family background.

However problematic this proved to be for someone who is inherently reluctant to talk about people or events which could possibly cause offence, in a work which considers parallel lives, honesty in comparisons is essential. Besides, *'writing'* about one's past provides not only the opportunity to overcome natural diffidence and lack of confidence in discussions, but also, and no less importantly, the opportunity to acquaint children with family history. My own children need to know what has made this old curmudgeon think, talk, and act as he does. They deserve to know more about his background and why and how people and events have shaped his life and made him so determined to speak out against hatred of the *'Other'*, and why he is so insistent about the importance of education – and reading, in particular - in combatting the virus of hatred and division.

For this reason, following the shock of Denis' sudden death, my own serious and debilitating bouts of sciatica brought on by a series of bulging discs in my back which impinge on the sciatic nerve, and the realisation that time was no longer on my side, I determined to reach into my memory bank while that was still possible and to record my recollections of some of those events which have had such an influence on my development as a person. As Jonathan Sumption so correctly states:

"We are all prisoners of our own experience".[2]

In particular I wanted to record the information I gleaned from the many conversations I have enjoyed with my Spanish, octogenarian friend, Luis Ramallo, whom I met some years ago in a bar in Mallorca. He it was who advised me to erase the word 'retirement' from my vocabulary as he had done. During these conversations – I should really refer to them as tutorials such was the mine of information and wisdom he passed on – I found myself comparing his background, wealth of knowledge and experience with my own comparatively limited educational and political background and life experience. Despite the differences in background and worldly experience, however, over the years we have become really good friends and are always in touch, either during our meetings in Mallorca, where we discuss the latest world news and set the world to right, or by phone when I want his opinion or information about some matter of import. In particular, our conversations would inevitably gravitate towards those differences between classes, races, religions and people in general which have so scarred humanity throughout the ages with such deadly and devastating effect and whether it is possible to reconcile historical differences. Given the apparent need for certain races, individuals or groupings to feel superior to people from different backgrounds and the readiness of some elements to exploit existing differences for their own ends, we were only too aware of the obstacles to reconciliation and co-existence.

Our discussions, based mainly on our own, often life-changing experiences, revolved around

---

[2] Jonathan Sumption: Trials of the State, Preface x

consideration of this *'Us and Them'* mentality as manifested in the fields of Education, Politics and Religion in the United States, Britain, Spain, Portugal, Chile, the Balkans, Ireland and Scotland. Of course, there are many other places where conflicts exist resulting from such differences, but these are the countries where Luis and I have experienced the adverse effects of intolerance of others.

Awakening

The mind is its own place and within it great distances can be imagined and traversed at will

Seamus Heaney

Every step I have taken outside my comfort zone, every new experience, every book I have read and every person I have met in life, all have challenged the certainty of ignorance. My beliefs, my views on topics such as education, politics and religion, for example, have been influenced by events and people and this on-going learning curve, which I refer to as a long awakening from ignorance, continues into my eightieth year. It was not easy for me to come to terms with the vital importance of education given my working-class background where, with rare exceptions, the norm was to leave school as soon as possible and to find employment. For the most part there was no understanding among my peers that:

"What saves is the willingness to learn from what you don't know. That is faith in the possibility of human transformation. That is faith in the sacrifice of the current self for the self that could be."[3]

---

[3] Jordan B Peterson: 12 Rules for Life

9

The more I read the more I understood how easily those who find it unnecessary to think or study or investigate can be manipulated. Politicians and their supporters in the media are not averse to playing members of the public against one another in order to gain support for particular, often controversial policies and are quite prepared to exploit fear, ignorance and bigotry as their tactic of first resort – anything goes. Labelling is a weapon used by politicians and populists, a crutch for the emotionally insecure, and a favourite tactic used by the so-called 'specialised' class to cause division among the *'herd'*. According to those on the far-right of British politics, for example, anyone expressing what they consider to be liberal or left-of-centre political views should automatically be considered dangerous and labelled as such. Labour Party politicians and trade union activists are particular targets for vilification by the right-wing press. Jeremy Corbyn, the former leader of the Labour Party has been a particular target for labelling, being alternatively referred to as 'Comrade' Corbyn or Jez the 'Red'; Ed Milliband, another former leader of the Labour Party was also referred to as 'Red' Ed when there was the possibility that he might become Prime Minister; and Ken Livingston, former Mayor of London was also frequently labelled 'Red' Ken. All this in a crude, but nevertheless all too often successful attempt to smear political opponents and influence voters.

Of course, in politics 'red-baiting' is nothing new. An import from the United States - it became a tactic among Republican candidates in the early 1950s during the McCarthy era – it re-emerges during every election as do descriptions such as *anti-American (or anti-British), anti-democratic, unpatriotic and* even *traitor* to attack opponents. Even Barack Obama was labelled a Marxist, anti-American and a secret Muslim. These were the tactics employed so successfully by Donald Trump during his campaign for the presidency. In Britain 'red-baiting' and charges of being anti-British and un-patriotic were constantly levelled against Jeremy Corbyn during the 2019 general election.

Not that those on the political left are entirely free from the charge of labelling opponents, particularly now that social media offers an alternative vehicle of communication to those on the left who wish to indulge in similar smear tactics. Nor is vitriol solely confined to opponents. Jewish members of the Labour Party have reported suffering anti-Semitic harassment from so-called comrades. The fact that their complaints were not taken seriously enough, and not seen to have been properly investigated, has resulted in serious divisions and a major problem for the Party. Indeed, failure to act timeously on the complaints led to the expulsion of the Party's former leader Jeremy Corbyn. Of course, the main target for labelling by those on the left are political opponents and so those who advocate serious debate about current immigration policies, health care provision or the benefits system invite charges of racism, hidden agendas or callous and inhumane disregard for the plight of the poorest members of society. The truth is that the electoral campaigns of too many politicians, and most political parties and activists, aim to exploit the ignorance and apathy of certain sections of the electorate by concentrating on their prejudices and fears. Labelling has proved a successful tactic in this regard.

Unfortunately, politicians and people in power know only too well that objectivity is not a concept understood by those whose thought processes have often been distorted by ignorance, fear or prejudice and who are only too ready to mimic attacks on opponents based on unsubstantiated claims of disloyalty or lack of patriotism, for example. Now, whenever I hear words like patriotism, loyalty, traitor or anti-British I am wary of the speaker's motives. Nor should it be assumed that labels are only used to discredit public figures. Too many people in the general public are influenced by the examples of labelling they come across in the media. Even though 'I am not now, nor have I ever been' a member of any political party which could remotely be described as subversive or a threat to national security I myself have at times been referred to as "Red Ed" - a tag frequently attached to anyone who thinks, or more accurately acts, even remotely outside the parameters of conventional politics.

It is true that I have been an active trade unionist all my life and in my position as Educational Institute of Scotland (EIS) union rep., among my so- called crimes I once had the temerity to explain the dangers posed by asbestos in public buildings and campaigned specifically for its removal from classrooms; to argue the case for an equal value rather than an equal opportunity philosophy in education; and for the importance of physical and social education to be given as much weight in the curriculum as more academic subjects (*mens sana in corpore sano*). All this much to the annoyance of some in authority. I have always encouraged members to support calls by the EIS for action to protect standards in education as well as living standards and working conditions - such support has often come at considerable financial cost to myself and my family - and, generally, have been a life-long supporter of workers' rights. I should also point out that I have had my critics on the political left and, more than once, have been disdainfully described by some of the more hard-line union members as one of those sell-out negotiators of the 'soft left' - whatever that might mean - for advocating a reasoned and pragmatic approach to the resolution of disputes. You can please some of the people some of the time.

However, the truth is, I am neither 'red' nor 'soft'. I am still a practising Catholic although in common with most adherents of any faith I have found it difficult, if not impossible, to live up to the tenets of Christianity - saints don't need to go on pilgrimages. If pressed I would probably describe myself as a 'questioning' Catholic. By that I mean I am no longer the boy who accepted without question some of the more extreme views which were drummed into me by some overzealous primary teachers – I once had my head rattled against a blackboard, not for missing Sunday Mass but for not receiving Holy Communion. These things stick with you. Nor am I that young man who decided not to attend my sister-in-law's wedding because she was marrying outside the Church – mixed marriages were frowned upon in those days, and still are by some, and not just by Catholics. That particular injunction has a long history, of course. One of the stipulations of the anti-Catholic Penal Laws of 1607 was that any children of a mixed marriage had to be brought up in the Protestant faith and in later years part of the oath taken by members of the Loyal Orange Institution of Ireland was to promise never to marry a Roman Catholic - most prejudices have their roots in the past. For my part, I have deeply regretted taking that decision to this day. All my children have partners who are not of my faith and I couldn't be happier for them. When I think that as a youth, I believed that missing Mass was not just a sin, but a mortal sin, I realise just how naïve and gullible I was. Nor was I alone. I recently had occasion to ask friends of a similar age and background for an example of a 'mortal' sin and to a man they parroted "missing Sunday Mass" - not nuclear war, murder, rape, paedophilia or corruption. That was the mentality of working-class Catholics in my early days. We lived in what I have already referred to as the certainty of ignorance.

Don't get me wrong! I still get comfort and solace from attending   Sunday mass and would only miss it through illness or travel difficulties, but should I miss it I would not feel compelled to rush to confession. Of course, people get their moral compass from different sources whether religious or non-religious, or more directly from their parents or circle of friends. As for me, whatever morals I have, and whatever positive influence these have had on my dealings with others, derive from that grounding in Catholicism, though I must admit to having singularly failed to live up to the commandments we are expected to live by. However, I have to confess that that same catholic education left me with many severe hang-ups which it has taken years, education and life-experience to partially overcome.

The long process of awaking from the social, political and religious cocoon of ignorance in which I spent my formative years is outlined in the following pages which highlight the influence various events and people have had on my political and social development. It was during the many discussions I have had with my Spanish friend and reflections on our life experience that we agreed that I should commit to print the effect particular events and experiences have had, not only on our lives, but also on the lives of others less fortunate than ourselves. During our many meetings, the conversation would inevitably return to the topic of those differences between classes, races, religions and people in general which have so scarred humanity down through the ages with such devastating and deadly effect. More importantly our thoughts would turn to the possibility, or indeed perhaps the impossibility, of reconciling such differences.

I do not expect the views expressed here to be universally accepted or indeed welcomed, after all they touch on some thorny issues. It has certainly not been my intention to offend but I am long enough in the tooth to realise that it is impossible to discuss controversial topics without causing offence to someone. However, to say nothing would be to ignore obvious injustices. If my comments provoke debate and stimulate reasoned discussion, they will have served my purpose. The Spaniards have a saying: !Quién calla otorga! He who is silent, consents.

Chapter 2

A Chance Encounter

"We all live in the hope that authentic meeting between humans can still occur"
R. D. Laing

Bar/Restaurante "Cala Canta" has become my local whenever I visit my daughter in Ciutat Jardi which lies on the coast a few kilometres east of Palma, capital city of Mallorca. The restaurant is ideally situated on the seafront, with magnificent views over Palma Bay and to the west Palma itself with its thirteenth century gothic Catedral de Santa María (begun in 1229 but not finished until 1601) and the gothic styled circular 14th century Bellver Castle which overlooks the Port area - both particularly prominent at night when illuminated.

The restaurant, situated on the corner site where Miquel Fullana Street meets Carrer Trafalgar, looks on to the golden sandy beach which stretches from Palma via Portixol, Molinar and beyond Ciutat Jardi, to Cala Gamba, C'an Pastilla as far as S'Arenal. Given its privileged position the Cala Canta is a favourite resting place for the many walkers - locals and tourists - who take advantage of the magnificent promenade, as well as for the constant stream of cyclists who avail themselves of the cycle path which runs parallel to the prom.

Whenever we are out of an evening, whether for a meal or a stroll, my wife and I like to round off our night on the terrace of the Cala Canta – Margaret with a decaf coffee and a cake of her choice and I with a coffee and "copita de 103". It was during one of our many evening visits, some years ago now, that I first noticed a distinguished looking, silver-haired gentleman sitting at a table in the corner of the restaurant on his own, sipping a glass of whisky and reading a fairly voluminous hard backed novel, his cane propped against the angle of the walls behind him, a supermarket shopping bag on the other empty chair at his table.

Initiating a conversation with a total stranger has never come easy to me, as Margaret, an outgoing and gregarious person herself, often reminds me. However, once I became aware of his presence as he sat reading at the same table in the corner of the front dining area every time I visited the Cala Canta of an evening, I determined to introduce myself to this kindred spirit – book lovers in these days of Twitter, Facebook and Instagram are becoming a rarer breed. Indeed, rather worryingly, even the former President of the most powerful country on earth tended to favour communication by twitter. That was my first meeting with D. Luis Ignacio Ramallo Massanet and so began a friendship which has continued to blossom over the years.

As time passed and we became firm friends and at ease in each other's company, Luis, who rarely spoke about himself, began to reveal details about his background and life experiences which I found more and more fascinating, details which not one of the many other diners could have imagined of this reserved, unpretentious elderly gentleman sitting in his 'office' absorbed in his latest reading material – he was equally at home reading Jules Verne's '20,000 Leagues Under the Sea' (Verne was one of his favourite authors) or dipping into Yaval Noah Harari's "Sapiens:

A Brief History of Humankind, Homo Deus".

A man well into his eighties, I have always been particularly impressed with his energy, enthusiasm and zest for life as he frequently flies from Palma to major provincial capitals to attend conferences and cultural events. Whenever I have occasion to phone him, I never know whether he will be at home in Ciutat Jardi or in Barcelona, Madrid or Las Palmas. The recent ITV series 'Joanna Lumley's Silk Road Adventures' brought to mind one such conference which he attended in 2015 at the age of eighty-four as President of the Spanish National Commission for Co-operation with UNESCO, the organisation which had arranged the event.

The three day conference held in Valencia in June, 2015, - the "Conferencia Internacional – Multaqa de las tres Culturas", the three cultures being |Islamic, Jewish and Christian – included lectures on 'The Silk Road between Asia, Europe and America'; ' The Silk Road as Migrant Heritage'; 'Silk cities in Spain and Europe: Some inspiring experiences in Cultural Heritage Management'; and 'Valencia on the Silk Roads'. All in all a heavy, energy sapping programme for a much younger person than this indefatigable octogenarian, yet this was but one of the many events and conferences he attends annually and even these events are but one facet of the life lived by this old "trotamundos".

The Cala Canta

"Labour preserves us from three great vices: Weariness, Vice and Want"

Voltaire: Candide

I recently had a discussion with Don Manuel Parra Martínez and his charming Dutch wife, Doña Hermanna Wörm, the long-time tenants of the Cala Canta, which provided me with some very interesting historical background, not only to the restaurant which they had run since 1971, but also to their own difficult background and the hard work and commitment they had put in over the years in order to ensure the restaurant's current success. As Don Manuel and Doña Hermanna are now retired, the day-to-day running of the restaurant is now left in the very capable hands of their son Juanman and his sister María de los Angeles and her husband Paco who take on the responsibility in alternate years. An interesting arrangement which seems to suit all concerned.

The youngest of ten children, Don Manuel, Manolo, was born in the little village of Rincón de Seca on the outskirts of Murcia in the South of Spain, 16 March 1936, the year of the outbreak of the Spanish Civil War, a time of great turmoil and suffering. His story perfectly illustrates how many ordinary people, so often the victims of wars over competing political systems over which they themselves have no control, find the spirit and courage to overcome seemingly insurmountable obstacles in order to survive and to prosper, even if that necessitates travelling far from their place of birth in order to do so.

According to what he was led to believe, Manolo was the last child to be baptised in his village church before it was destroyed by anti-clerical Republican forces. Unfortunately, in the years following the Nationalist victory six of Manolo's siblings died. These were years of famine and misery for ordinary people. There were no medicines and very little money. Those who were unfortunate enough to fall gravely ill were often destined to succumb to their illness. If there was no work, there was no money and starvation followed. Whatever money Manuel's father had been able to save was in Republican currency which had no value after the fall of the Republican Government. The family was penniless.

When he was 13, now an orphan, Manuel was taken to Mallorca by an older sister, now dead. His early years on the island were spent working alongside his sister in one of the most famous restaurante/pastelerías on the island, the "Riscal" in Palma, where his propensity for hard work and his open and friendly nature seem to have been much appreciated by his colleagues. He later worked in the Hotel Balear in the Plaza Mayor in Palma, which no longer exists, and the Hotel Neptuna in C'an Pastilla. In 1961 he took over the lease of the Bar Manolo which was located in Calle Trafalgar, practically on the seafront in Ciudat Jardi, which he successfully managed until 1971 when the owner decided that control of the business should pass on to his son and so refused to renew the lease.

Fortunately for Manuel he was friendly with the leaseholder of the Hostal Cala Canta - which was also located in Trafalgar Street - who had decided to retire. Since none of his children were anxious to take over the business he agreed to speak to the owner of the premises, D. Juan Mas Mascaró with whom he was on good terms and to recommend that Manuel take over the lease, which he duly did. In those days the Cala Canta was a really old building which, according to Manuel, had probably been a private house at some time during the 1930s/40s. As guest houses go it wasn't the most salubrious of venues and from a business point of view not the most viable but Manuel and Hermanna were determined to make a success of this new challenge.

Hermanna had met Manuel in the Bar Manolo in 1961 and they had married in 1966. A physical education teacher in Holland, she had contracted severe rheumatism at the age of 19 and was advised by her doctors that she would have to give up her teaching job and indeed think about moving to a country with a warmer climate. That advice took her to Mallorca and marriage to Manuel. She smiles when recounting an incident in hospital in Amsterdam where one day a fellow- patient, who insisted that she had been born with a gift for foretelling the future, advised Hermanna that she would marry, but would have to cross the sea to find a husband.

Not long after they took over the lease of the Cala Canta, they decided to convert the Hostal into a small family restaurant and both worked tirelessly to make a success of their new venture. During the day Hermanna would work in the restaurant while Manuel worked on old houses which they purchased with a view to renovation before letting or selling on. In the evening, once his day shift working on the houses was over, he would join his wife in the restaurant. During the winter, when the restaurant closed for three months, Manuel would concentrate on these renovation projects. By dint of their tireless efforts, over the years business thrived and gave them and their growing family a comfortable living, while at the same time providing employment for fourteen staff members, the perfect meeting and eating place for a couple of old friends and the ideal pit-stop for the many tourists of all nationalities who flocked to the area during the tourist season.

Catching up with the news and an early morning coffee at the Cala Canta

Chapter 3

Education

To learn without thinking is fruitless. To think without learning is dangerous.
                                        Confucius

During the many conversations I had with Luis I quickly became aware of the educational, social and experiential gulf between us. While we are both avid readers and often lament the fact that too many young people seem to have abandoned books in favour of social media, I have to admit that growing up I rarely if ever read a book. Indeed, I clearly remember my Professor of Spanish at Glasgow University remarking during a lecture that he had recently visited a house where there were no books. It immediately flashed through my mind that he could be describing the situation in my parents' house as well as in the homes of all of my close friends and, indeed, of the majority of poor working-class families.

Luis came from a different, more privileged background in which reading would be the norm from an early age. It was not until I began to experience life beyond my working class environment that I gradually came to understand the limitations of my vocabulary and life experience and to the realisation that my limited education put me at an enormous social disadvantage which resulted in a lack of confidence and even embarrassment at times when out of my comfort zone.

It was only when reading became an important part

of my life that I came to realise that one of the most striking differences between people from a privileged background and those from the working classes is the importance placed by the former on education. It is no coincidence that most lawmakers, politicians, and media moguls - the people who really shape our society - come from privileged backgrounds and have enjoyed the benefits of a private education. Too many working-class parents, even today, still fail to realise the importance of a well-rounded education. Their dismissive attitude toward anything remotely cultural rubs off on their children with the result that many pupils set their sights too low and so never reach their true potential. It has always been my belief that while preparing pupils for the workforce is important, the real purpose of education should always be to develop independent, inquiring minds - minds which are not prepared to accept without corroboration everything which is said or written.

Things have improved somewhat over the past decades, of course, and there are men and women from poorer backgrounds who, by dint of sheer hard work and dedication to study, have bucked the trend. But they are still in the minority. Power, by and large, lies in the hands of the privileged few and in political terms, when in government, with the backing of like-minded privileged people in big business and the media, they maintain themselves in power in a democracy by offering just enough to a sufficient number of the electorate to retain that power. For that reason, it is so important to take nothing as gospel, to question everything, to have an inquiring mind and to give rein to the imagination.

When I look back on my early years, long before half-truths, false rumours, lies and fake news made it even more impossible to distinguish fact from fiction, most of us believed that we in the West were on the side of the angels, that our priests, ministers, politicians and all those who had power over us would actively strive for a more just world. We had no notion of the duplicity of many of those in whom we put our trust. We knew little or nothing about paedophile priests and ministers, venal and corrupt politicians and press barons who use their power and influence to ensure that the privileges of the élite are protected from the growing demands of the "herd" and who hold up to ridicule those who challenge the gross inequalities in our communities, dismissing them as economic illiterates, naïve and dangerous.

Whenever Luis and I get together the absolute importance of education is frequently discussed and, not surprisingly, as we were both teachers, we are in total agreement on the subject, although we may differ at times as to how best to achieve the goal of providing an education the aim of which is to encourage independent, enquiring minds. These possible differences of approach to teaching are not surprising given that our own social and educational backgrounds could not have been more dissimilar though we were both educated by Religious Brothers.

I was born and raised in a poor working-class district in the East End of Glasgow, the youngest of five siblings. My father was killed in a mining accident when I was nine years old which left my mother the onerous and unenviable task of providing for my older sister and me on her own with little financial assistance to supplement her meagre wage as a Home Help and part-time cleaner. Two brothers and a sister, the eldest of the siblings, were married and out of the house by this time and had their own families to look after.

St Michael's Primary School which I attended from the age of five was only a stone throw from where I lived in Parkhead and there I was fortunate enough to achieve the requisite grade in the qualifying exam – the *Qualy* as we called it – to allow me to continue my education at St Mungo's Academy, the nearest senior secondary school, where I was taught by Brothers of the Marist Order. There was no comprehensive education in those days of course. Depending on the grade a pupil achieved in the qualifying exam he or she would go to the nearest junior or senior secondary school, the latter for pupils thought to be sufficiently clever to benefit from an academic education, the former for a more vocational education. The problem with that system was that many academically gifted pupils who were late developers or who had not performed at their best in the qualifying exam were labelled at the age of twelve. The attitude to education of many working-class parents and their children was exemplified by my eldest brother's decision to abandon his studies at St Mungo's Academy in order to transfer to the local Junior Secondary school, *'because he would be able to play football there.'* No such decision would have been countenanced by upper-class parents.

Given the economic circumstances at home, although I performed well academically at the Academy there was no prospect of me continuing my education beyond the age of sixteen – the earliest legal leaving age. As soon as the school became aware of this Brother Clare, the Marist Brother who was Headmaster at the time, summoned me to his office where I was lectured on the foolishness of my decision and the negative affect it would have on my future. He was correct of course as I was later to discover. However, when he failed to convince me of the many

26

benefits of continuing my studies, I was immediately transferred from the top language class in the year to make way for a pupil with a bit more sense.

With my mother having to take on two jobs to make ends meet I convinced myself, against her wishes, that I had to make a financial contribution and so, instead of studying to become a lawyer, teacher or doctor as Brother Clare insisted I should be working towards, I ended up packing goods in a warehouse for the meagre sum of £2 per week - a paltry contribution to the family income. Later I joined my brothers working shifts labouring in a non-ferrous foundry which at least allowed me to make a reasonable economic contribution. Work in the foundry was physically demanding and the fume-filled sheds, especially when the metal was being cast from the furnaces, was particularly damaging to health. Masks, and the milk issued to the men working in the lead plant, were pitifully inadequate to the task of protecting the health of workers. My own stint in the foundry resulted in a permanent weakness to my chest and lungs, leaving me vulnerable to infection. For that reason, I have had to be particularly careful and hygiene-aware ever since, especially during the covid-19 pandemic. Some of those who worked with me in the foundry, especially those who operated the furnace in the lead plant, most of whom had never even heard of lead poisoning, have not been fortunate enough to have survived as long as I have.

Those three years or so spent working in what we came to refer to as the 'Black hole of Calcutta' introduced me to the university of life, an education, inasmuch as it had a formative effect on my social and political attitudes. One of the first lessons I learned in that environment was that uninterrupted production and profit were more important to management and employers than health and safety. Certainly, during a time when there were few legal obligations to ensure safety in the workplace, the workers themselves had a 'gallus', macho disregard for basic commonsense precautions which could have gone some way to mitigate the worst aspects of conditions in the foundry. Masks were only ever worn during casting and sometimes not even then, inadequate footwear offered little protection from the inevitable spillage of moulting metal during casting and little thought was given to the danger from the overhead cranes constantly transferring skips of metal to be used in the furnaces.

Still a teenager, lacking the self-confidence of the well-educated or the bravado, arrogance and swagger of some of the other workers, it took me two years to pluck up the courage to approach management with a view to negotiating an increase in my basic wage - a seminal decision as it turned out. The paltry, insulting, take it or leave offer I received was instrumental in my taking the decision to embark on a completely different career path. The offer was of an increase of one half-pence per hour, or twenty pence for a forty-hour week, and that only after a long explanation of how difficult things were for everyone from a man with the latest, brand new Jaguar car sitting in the car park. I accepted the offer but there and then determined that never again would I be treated with such disdain. I learned two things that day,

a) that maximising profit is everything in business which means wages must be kept at a level commensurate with profit targets, and,

b) workers trying to negotiate wages or conditions for themselves as individuals is exactly how employers like to operate.

However, that miserable offer was the best thing my employer could have done for me. It made me realise the importance of education. It was only then that I finally appreciated what Brother Clare had tried to warn me about the consequences of leaving school without completing my studies. My renewed interest in education took me via a correspondence course and evening classes to a place at Glasgow University where I studied French, Spanish, Portuguese and Latin American Studies, graduating with Honours. An integral part of my degree course was the requirement to spend time in the countries whose language I was studying and so in consecutive years I enrolled in courses at the Universities of Madrid, Coimbra and Caen.

I had always wanted to experience the world outside my working-class cocoon, to experience other cultures, to visit other countries and so this was a wonderful opportunity although what I found at times clashed with my growing politically left leaning views. This was at a time when Spain, following the cessation of hostilities in the Spanish Civil war, was ruled between 1939 and 1975 by the dictator General Francisco Franco Bahamonde, an anti-democrat who was violently opposed to Communism, Masonry and Jewry. At the same time Portugal was experiencing the longest right-wing dictatorship in Europe under the rule of the ultra-conservative Antonio de Oliveira Salazar who was named Prime Minister by General Antonio Oscar de Fragoso Carmona in July 1932, a post he held until 1968. Like Franco he too was anti-democratic and opposed to communism, socialism, anarchism and Liberalism. In Caen, a port city in the Calvados department of Normandy, on the other hand,

I learned more about the sacrifices made to protect democracy during the D-Day 1944 Normandy landings. Visits to Omaha Beach and war-graves cemeteries with their serried lines of white crosses with the names of young men, many just teenagers, left me with an indelible impression of the madness and futility of a war, like most wars, fought on the one side to impose and on the other to prevent the imposition of an alien way of life.

Luis's Educational Background

He that acts by intelligence and cultivates understanding, is likely to be best disposed and dearest to God.

Aristotle

Luis's educational background differs greatly from my own, although there are one or two similarities – we were both educated by Brothers of Religious Orders and both experienced life under military dictatorships. It should be said, however, that Luis was actually living in Spain during the Civil War and in Chile when the democratically elected socialist government of Salvador Allende was overthrown by a United States, CIA-backed coup d'état on 11 September 1973. His experiences, especially in Chile, sometimes put him in great danger whereas I simply felt uncomfortable at times experiencing life in countries with political systems which were alien to me and contrary to my own incipient left leaning political views.

Born in Mallorca in 1931, five years before the outbreak of the Spanish Civil War, Luis Ignacio Ramallo Massanet first attended the Montesion College (El Colegio de Nuestra Señora de Montesion de Palma) the oldest functioning Jesuit college in the world which has been in existence for 450 years having been founded by Jesuits who arrived in Palma with the intention of setting up a college where young men training to become Jesuits could study. Apart from some short interludes when the Jesuit Order was out of favour in Spain the college has been in existence to the present day.

Luis's birth year coincided with the passing of the Second Republic's Constitution which decreed in Articles 24 and 26 that there should be strict controls on Church property and that religious orders should be prohibited from engaging in education - the inclusion of these two controversial articles led to the resignation of the conservative catholic republicans Alcalá-Zamora and Miguel Moura who tried unsuccessfully to oppose their introduction. The decrees relating to religious orders applied, in particular, to the Society of Jesus which was declared to be "disbanded and deprived of all juridical personality" within the territories of the Republic. As a consequence, the Jesuits responsible for the education of students at the Montesion College, on 2nd February 1932 had to abandon their places of residence and were dispersed to different houses in Palma.

However, when on 17/18 July, 1936, Generals Mola, Franco and Queipo de Llano led a military coup against the legally elected Republican Government in Madrid, the military on the Balearic Islands - Mallorca, Ibiza and Formentera - threw in their lot with the rebels and, despite a failed attempt to drive the rebel military forces out of Mallorca by an expeditionary Republican force at the Battle of Mallorca - sometimes referred to as the Mallorca Landings – the island remained under Nationalist control throughout the period of the Spanish Civil War.

Mallorca now being firmly in Nationalist hands, responsibility for the education of students at Montesion College was returned to the Jesuit Order. News of this decision was communicated to the dispersed members of the Order by the Civil Governor of the Balearics on the 29th October 1936 and classes resumed two years later when, on 10th October 1938, 120 students were in attendance. Luis Ramallo by this time would have been of an age to be included among the first students to attend classes following the hiatus during the Second Republic.

There being no university in Palma – the University of Palma did not open until 1975 – Luis was forced to leave the Island to continue his education at the Monasterio de Veruela (Real Monasterio de Santa María de Veruela) situated near Vera de Moncayo, a municipality in the Province of Zaragoza, which although founded originally in 1145 by the Cistercian Order, by the time Luis arrived it had been in the hands of the Jesuits since 1875 and remained so until 1975. After four years studying for his Baccalaureate, reluctant to continue his studies in Franco's Spain, he went as a volunteer with the Jesuits to Paraguay where he learned Guarani, the local Indian language, which he later taught to the Jesuit students and volunteers who came after him.

After more than a decade in Paraguay his Jesuit sponsor and advisor, Father Julián Sayos, advised him not to return to Spain but to further his education at the Pontifical Xaverian University, La Javeriana, in Bogotá, Colombia, one of the oldest - founded in 1623 – and most prestigious of Colombia's universities where Colombia's élite has traditionally been educated. After four very happy years at La Javeriana, he received a bachelor's degree in philosophy of

Science and Education. Father Sayos then arranged with some friends in the United States to send him to study theology at the privately run Jesuit Weston College in Boston which in 1967 merged with Boston College following which, for the first time, Weston matriculated students who were not members of the Jesuit order. Such was the prestige enjoyed by Boston College that it counted among its former students such names as John Kerry, former U.S Secretary of State and unsuccessful candidate for the Presidency, Tip O'Neill former Speaker of the U.S House of Representatives, Ken Hackett former ambassador to the Vatican and Steve Barry Managing Director of Goldman Sachs and Co. as well as other notable public figures. If he ever came into contact with any of the College's notable alumni Luis never referred to them during the many discussions we had about his time in Boston. It isn't his style. After four years Luis took Holy Orders and was ordained by the then Archbishop of Boston, Richard Cushing, who as Cardinal Cushing gave the invocation at President Kennedy's inauguration.

While still in Boston a scholarship from the Organisation of American States (Organización de Estados Americanos), petitioned by Paraguay, allowed him to begin a four year course at Harvard University in Cambridge, Massachusetts which led to a Doctorate in Social Psychology after which he returned to Paraguay to teach at the Universidad de Nuestra Señora de la Asunción. There he was instrumental with other colleagues in introducing reforms which led to the introduction of the Faculty of Psychology and the Centre of Investigation and Social Action. His work at the University in Asunción brought him to the attention of UNESCO and he was given a temporary contract to take up a post of visiting expert in Social Sciences at the University of Sao Paola in Brazil - duties which he fulfilled while still based in Asunción. He was then contracted by UNESCO to a post in Santiago de Chile where he became Director of the Latin American School of Sociology which was attached to the Latin American Faculty of Social Sciences (FLACSO), a posting which suited him greatly as he enjoyed much more freedom, being neither subject to the Archbishop of Asunción nor the Rector of the University but rather assigned to UNESCO.

By this time, he was becoming less and less involved in priestly duties and, since he now found his lay work more fulfilling, he eventually approached the Jesuit General, Father Pedro Arrupe, to explain that he wished to be laicized. Although Father Arrupe accepted that Luís's life now mostly involved non-religious duties he, personally, had no authority to laicize. However, he did advise Luis that he would have to write to the Vatican directly, seeking permission to be relieved of his priestly duties and assisted him in presenting the case for laicization which was eventually granted.

Luis was now free to concentrate on his work as a staff member and consultant with UNESCO, serving two terms representing Spain on the Executive Council. He chaired the Spanish National Commission for Cooperation with UNESCO, served as President of the Executive Council's Group of Experts on Administrative and Treasury matters, and carried out multiple technical missions – he was the Director General of UNESCO's personal representative for all matters relating to the former Yugoslavia in which capacity he participated in efforts to re-establish peace in Bosnia Herzegovina and to prevent war in Kosovo.

Chapter 4

A Political Education – Events at Home

Time moves in one direction, memory another
William Gibson

Most people are apolitical by nature. They have no interest in politics and little or no trust in politicians. The general perception is that no matter which party or candidate people give their vote to, little will change which will materially improve their lot. The apathy of electorates and this mistrust of traditional parties has given rise to populism and the emergence of politicians whose principal *raison d'etre* is to sweep away the old political order. Their tactic is to appeal to the emotions of the people by offering simplistic solutions to complex economic and social problems - not that this is an entirely new approach to politics.

Traditional parties have for far too long taken the electorate for granted, assuming that the people will forever suffer with equanimity the persistent disregard for what they consider to be the real social and economic problems which they face in their daily lives. The decade long politics of austerity introduced as a result of a banking crash, which started first in America, due among other things, to an over-zealous reliance on sub-prime lending after Richard Nixon had rolled back Roosevelt's New Deal regulations, was a classic example of how, in a crisis, it is the ordinary people who shoulder the greatest burden. It did not go unnoticed by the population at large that, while ordinary people were being expected to tighten their belts to help tackle a national debt which they were in no way responsible for, the richest percentile of the community was becoming progressively richer.

Callousness with regard to, and disregard for, the well-being of certain sections of the population is nothing new of course. It has always been the case. One has only to look back over the twentieth century to find examples of the contempt the élite has for the "lower orders". Of course the media in Western countries would have us believe that this is only the norm in dictatorships and so we are not surprised to read, for example, that the Portuguese authoritarian Antonio de Oliveira Salazar, whose Estado Novo Government ruled Portugal between 1932 to 1974, believed that *"the Portuguese must be treated as children, too much too often would spoil them"* – a view echoed by the Portuguese 'leitora' who was one of my tutors at the University of Glasgow. In her opinion children as young as twelve should be out working. Of course, the truth is that the same contempt for the general population is also pervasive in so-called democratic countries.

Walter Lippman (1889-1974), regarded by many as the dean of American journalists, believed that *"the common interests elude public opinion entirely"* and can only be managed by a *"specialised class of responsible men"*.

A similar sentiment was echoed by Harold Dwight Lasswell (1902–1978), a leading political scientist and communication theorist who shared the belief that:

"We should not succumb to democratic dogmatisms about men being the best judges of their own interests, because they're not. Therefore, just out of ordinary morality, we have to make sure that they don't have the

opportunity to act on the basis of their misjudgements."[4]

Lasswell went on to argue that, since most people are guided by emotion and impulse, those who have rationality have to create *"necessary illusions and emotionally potent simplifications"*[5] in order to keep the naïve simpletons more or less on the same course. In other words, we have to "manufacture consent" – *"Propaganda is to democracy what the bludgeon is to a totalitarian state."*[6]

The problem arises for the élite when the "simpletons" are given too little for too long and either take to the streets as they do regularly in France, as President Macron found to his cost recently with the demonstrations in the centre of Paris by *'les gilets jaunes',* against the rise in fuel tax in particular, and as a result of the general discontent over long years of austerity. Alternatively, they threaten the democratic status quo by voting for populist parties or candidates, as has happened in the United States, Brazil and several countries in Europe. People tend to become politicised by events either in their own individual or collective experiences or when their own particular interests are threatened. Some, by dint of self-education, even have the temerity to think for themselves and come to reject and to challenge received political wisdom.

The road to my own political Damascus began 14 April 1949 when I was only nine years old. On that day my father was killed at the Fireclay Pit, Heathfield, Chryston in Lanarkshire. His death certificate put it bluntly:

---

[4] Noam Chomsky: Media Control, p20
[5] Ibid., p20
[6] Noam Chomsky: Media Control, pp20/21

"While engaged in his employment as a clay miner's drawer the deceased was engaged at the mine face loading a hutch when a fall of stone from the roof weighing about one and a half hundred weights fell on him whereby he sustained a fractured skull from which he died, as above. As per Finding of Jury." Case closed.

My mother thought otherwise. In a letter to the mine owners she queried how such an accident could have happened so soon after the safety officer had inspected the mine - just before my father started his early morning shift. She was not convinced that the mine had been inspected that morning. Without proof of course she could do no more than voice her reservations. However, instead of sympathising with a bereaved widow and perhaps explaining that accidents can happen even after inspections – if the inspection did indeed take place that day – someone at the company felt it necessary to send a motorcycle policeman to warn her against any further communications. The fact that a policeman - who had no jurisdiction in Glasgow - was sent on such a mission indicated to me, even at such a young age, that this was a clear case of intimidation. The policeman himself was highly embarrassed at having been placed in such a situation. Someone obviously feared that my mother would file a claim against the company which she never did. I have never forgotten that incident, not only because of the effect it had on my mother, but also because when I saw the policeman I immediately assumed that he was the bearer of distressing news about my eldest sister who was seriously ill in hospital with tuberculosis at the time. That was my first experience of the Us and Them divisions in society which are the cause of so much strife in the world.

Manifestations of the social divisions in our society can be much more subtle of course. Even decent, well-meaning people can unwittingly offend or cause embarrassment. When I finally arrived at Glasgow University as a mature student, I was apprehensive and somewhat intimidated by my surroundings. While I probably had more experience of life than most of the students with whom I came in contact, I was acutely aware of the gaps in my education. When my lecturer in Brazilian Studies became aware of my working-class background, he rather condescendingly remarked that I had done well to "get out of it." My first reaction was one of disappointment. Here was someone I had respected. He was a good teacher and a pleasant and very amiable individual, but did he think that I was ashamed of my background? Did he think that I could forget my widowed mother's struggle to keep a roof over our head, having to rely at times on state handouts despite working two jobs, while at the same time having to make long daily journeys to care for a seriously ill daughter who lived miles from our home? How could I possibly forget the sacrifices made by a pregnant wife who, with a full-time job was still able to manage our home and look after two children while I continued my studies in Portugal, London and Caen? Without her moral and financial support I would never have been able to continue my studies at the university. Thinking back about my tutor's comment, I'm sure there was no intention to offend but one thing I have learned after years of avid reading: it is crucially important to be careful with words. Once spoken they can never be fully retracted or forgotten. Between the thought and the word there is so much room for often damaging misinterpretation.

Once qualified as a secondary school teacher of

French and Spanish, it was not long before I became involved, firstly with the EIS, the largest of Scotland's teachers' unions and then with the Scottish Labour Party, in the hope of making some small contribution to the fight against the ravages of Thatcherism. Despite my best efforts, however, after almost ten years in both organisations I had to admit that reconciling differences between factions was so difficult as to be well-nigh impossible at times. However, while we are all of us the product of our environment to a greater or lesser extent, I have learned over the years that it is possible to bridge social divides, as Luis and I have done so well over the years. All that is required is to jettison egos, preconceived ideas and class misconceptions – not easy I admit, as I have found to my frustration at times. Unfortunately, the problem is not confined to class differences. Even within the same social groupings or organisations it is not uncommon to come across racial or religious prejudices, which in extreme cases betray an underlying mistrust and even hatred for particular individuals or factions in a community.

Unfortunately, too many people see what they want to see, hear what they want to hear and believe what they have been conditioned to believe from birth. Objectivity is not a concept understood by those whose mind has been closed to alternative points of view and whose thinking is distorted by ignorance, fear, prejudice or dismissal of '*the Other*.' Nowhere is this more prevalent than in the West of Scotland. Go to any football match between the two Glasgow giants, Celtic and Rangers and you will hear the most vile and vicious insults being exchanged between rival fans. It has been my experience on more than one occasion that in these extreme cases any attempt to overcome differences, to promote understanding of another's point of view or to advocate compromise, is regarded almost as a betrayal of one's friends or heritage.

A prime example of the latter was the failure of my attempt to overcome the poisonous atmosphere between factions of the same Constituency Labour Party of which I was member. Such was the often vitriolic animosity between so-called comrades, at a time when we should have been concentrating our attention on opposing the Thatcher Government, that I felt obliged to write to the late John Smith, the then Labour Party Leader and Constituency MP, to seek his intervention. His reply, dated 22nd March 1988, which recognised the existence of a problem, contained, as I expected, a reassurance that he would continue to do what he could to help heal divisions although in terms of the constitution he was unable to directly interfere in constituency affairs. My hope was that his intervention would prove more successful than were my own efforts, but I was not altogether confident that even one as respected as John could heal the rift between different factions within the Party. After all, disputes between members of political parties and indeed within most organisations are not uncommon. Certainly nothing much has changed within the Labour Party even today, as witness the splits over the Party's approach to the whole Brexit issue and the bitter disputes between pro and anti-Corbyn factions during the latter's leadership.

I had not expected John to make a public attempt to heal the rifts between members, but I thought it might have been possible to knock a few heads together behind the scenes. He probably thought, as I did, that to bring some sanity back to the situation within the Constituency Party required the wisdom of Solomon and the patience of Job. Wisdom he had in abundance but as Leader of the opposition, with so much on his plate, I had wondered whether he would have had the time to exercise the necessary patience to involve himself in petty squabbles between local party members and their less than comradely machinations.

Politics is a dirty business as I was forcibly reminded by a journalist when I allowed my name to be put forward, with others, as a candidate to fill the vacant position of M.P. for Monklands East when John died, 12 May 1994. "Fighting an election is like being thrown into a bear pit. It can be dehumanising", I was warned. As it transpired the selection panel decided that there was a more suitable candidate to confront the bruising cut and thrust of what turned out to be a particularly nasty bye-election. When it comes to elections there are no holds barred and even normally decent individuals can be drawn into murky waters.

1984: The Miners' Strike

Past events it is argued have no objective existence but survive only in written records and in human memories.
George Orwell: 1984

The 1984/85 Miners strike was another key event which had a profound influence not only on myself as someone who knew at first hand the dangers faced by miners on a daily basis but also on the majority of working people who recognised that, if any group could stand against Thatcher's messianic onslaught on workers' pay and conditions and against mass redundancies, it would be the miners. Unfortunately, Thatcher, who regarded the miners as "the enemy within", recognised this too and her government,

42

committed to destroying 'militant' trade unionism, was well prepared for the coming unequal struggle. According to her biographer Charles Moore, no sooner had she taken office in 1979 when she called in Willie Whitelaw and told him that there would be another miners' strike but that this time the government would win. She was advised by the Whitehall Contingency Unit that any strike should begin in spring and that it should be over pit closures, which tended to divide the union, rather than about pay, which tended to unite workers. In 1977, seven years before the government was ready to implement it, Nicholas Ridley devised a strategy to defeat the miners. This included the stockpiling of coal, increasing power-station capacity to switch from coal to oil, the use of non-union haulage drivers and cuts in supplementary benefit to strikers' families. Thatcher revealed in her memoirs that Ian McGregor, appointed National Coal Board (NCB) Chairman in 1983, had a secret plan to cut 75,000 jobs in three years. Arthur Scargill, the National Union of Mineworkers (NUM) leader, had underestimated the number of job losses.

If one incident during the strike epitomised the mismatch in terms of the forces ranged against the miners it occurred at Orgreave, a small village on the River Rother in South Yorkshire. The Battle of Orgreave, as it has come to be known, was a vicious confrontation on 18 June 1984 between police and pickets at a British Steel Corporation coking plant in Orgreave which led to 95 people being arrested, 71 charged with riot and 24 with violent disorder. At the time riot was punishable by life imprisonment. However, all the charges were subsequently dropped amid questions about the reliability of police evidence. In June 1991, South Yorkshire Police paid £425,000 in compensation to 39 miners for assault, wrongful arrest, unlawful detention and malicious prosecution.

Afterwards the Independent Police Complaints Commission stated, following a review of documentation, that there was evidence of perjury by police officers in the prosecution of miners, and a cover-up afterwards, but that it could not investigate further due to the passage of time. Scant regard had been given to the affect these prosecutions would have on the lives of those arrested on trumped up charges. Theresa May, to her credit, invited calls for an inquiry, pointing out that:

"We must never underestimate how the poison of decades-old misdeeds seeps down through the years and is just as toxic today as it was then. That's why difficult truths, however unpalatable they may be, must be confronted head-on."[7]

That prescient warning was subsequently ignored by her own government.

Why have the events that took place at Orgreave that day left such a bitter legacy that many trade unionists still remember the police as "Maggie's Boot Boys" and still mistrust the force even today, just as Theresa May predicted would happen in her speech to the Police Federation? The answer lies in the tactics employed by the police to defeat the miners at Orgreave as described in the following extract from an article which appeared in The Irish Times, Tuesday December 18, 2018:

"During the 1984 strike, police had usually prevented...pickets from converging by blocking them along the way but the pickets arrived at Orgreave

---

[7] Theresa May addressing the Police Federation Annual Conference, 17 May 2016

without difficulty. They were allowed to assemble close to the coke works before police moved them into an open field, where they were surrounded by 4,500 officers. When the first strike-breaking lorries appeared, the striking miners pushed forward against police lines. But instead of resisting, the lines parted to allow mounted police to charge the miners, who responded by throwing stones. When the BBC showed the scene on television, it reversed the sequence, so that it appeared the mounted charge was a response to the stone-throwing."[8]

Short-shield police units moved in, bludgeoning miners over the head and body, sometimes wearing boiler suits rather than police uniforms having first removed identification numbers. The general suspicion, indeed, the firm belief among miners, was that the police had planned the confrontation. A senior police officer came close to admitting as much and David Hart, a businessman who advised Thatcher during the strike, was even blunter, when he admitted in 1993 that:

"The coke was of no interest whatsoever. We didn't need it. It was a battleground of our choosing on grounds of our choosing ....The fact is that it was a set-up and it worked brilliantly,"[9]

As much as the Media and government would have had us believe that the country was saved from a communist inspired plot to destabilise the government, and not to save thousands of jobs as the miners asserted, when the facts became clear and the real plotters were uncovered, the public at large refused to accept the scurrilous charge that the miners were "the

---

[8] The Irish Times, Tuesday December18, 2018
[9] David Conn: Burning Injustice of Orgreave is left Burning

enemy within." Whether you agreed with the NUM's tactics or not - and things may have been different had there been a National Ballot for strike action - even opponents of the strike couldn't help but admire the fortitude and solidarity of the mining communities involved in a dispute during which whole families suffered harassment, hardship and hunger for a full year. Not that the most zealous of Thatcher's supporters would agree, of course. Just as she congratulated the police on a job well done, they extolled the praises of the 'Iron Lady' who to their way of thinking, in breaking the unions, saved the country from anarchy.

However, one thing you have to admit, if not admire, about Margaret Thatcher is that she looked after the interests of her privileged backers.

"By the end of the Tories reign in 1996, the richest 10% of families with three children were £21,000 richer on average than when Thatcher came to power. In contrast a family with three children in the bottom 10% of the population was £625 poorer than when she arrived at No 10."[10]

Among the worst to suffer through job losses were the mining communities. Of the 247,000 mining jobs in 1976 only 44,000 remained by 1993 and as few as 2,000 by 2015.

Had the real reason for closing mines been to cut down the use of fossil fuels in the light of the potentially catastrophic global warming effect of climate change, and closures had been introduced over a number of years in order to plan alternative employment for redundant miners, so minimising social unrest and hardship, the closures might not have

---

[10] Owen Jones: Chavs

met with such violent resistance. However, that was not the case. Climate change was not in the forefront of the political agenda in 1984. Breaking the power of the unions, and Milton Friedman's free market trinity of privatisation, deregulation and cuts to social spending were the order of the day and Margaret Thatcher followed her guru's policies with relish.

The rapid progress in the field of artificial intelligence, automation and robotics will result inevitably, and in the not too distant future, in changes to jobs and society which will be in marked contrast to anything experienced, not only by the 1984 striking miners but also by most present day workers. Darrell M West, director of the centre for technology innovation at the Brookings Institution goes as far as to predict that there will be:

"limited full-time employment opportunities other than for workers such as coders, computer experts, designers and data scientists."[11]

Very few jobs will be safe, although low-skilled, low-paid jobs are most at risk. If we are to avoid social unrest on a much greater scale than that which accompanied the Thatcher government's determination to break the NUM and decimate employment in the coal industry, once and for all, we had better handle the transition to digital-based employment with considerably more compassion, foresight and understanding.

Never was there a greater need for far-sighted innovators capable of anticipating, addressing and preparing possible solutions to these inevitable changes in the world of work. Plans have to be made

---

[11] Darrel M West: The Future of Work: Robots, AI, and Automation

now if we are to minimise the future, negative social consequences of such radical technological changes to employment practices, especially since the world will have to confront at the same time the impending loss of employment in the oil and gas industries as it makes the transition to a green economy.

Chapter 5

A Lesson in Spanish History

Although in my conscience I needed no amnesty, for I had done nothing wrong, yet I was forced to think of myself as a criminal in hiding awaiting a pardon.
Ronald Fraser: In Hiding

My political education continued at the University of Madrid. Courses began in October 1966, a time when Spain was still ruled by the dictator General Francisco Franco. As a Scot and a student of Spanish History and Language I had studied the events leading up to the Civil war and had read accounts of the actual fighting by fellow Scots who had joined the International Brigades and fought in the battles of Jarama and Bruñete. Their descriptions of the horrors of war, as they witnessed the slaughter of the majority of their comrades at Bruñete, should be made compulsory reading for all those who advocate war as a way of settling differences.

Although the Spanish Civil War ended in 1939, during the year I spent in the Spanish capital I frequently came across evidence of the effect that brutal war and its aftermath still had on the Spanish people. Not that I should have been surprised:

"Behind the lines during the Spanish Civil War, nearly 200,000 men and women were murdered extra-judicially or executed after flimsy legal process .....perhaps as many as 200,000 men died at the battle fronts..... In all of Spain after the final victory of the rebels at the end of March 1939, approximately 20,000

Republicans were executed. Many more died of disease and malnutrition in overcrowded unhygienic prisons and concentration camps.......More than half a million refugees were forced into exile and many were to die in French concentration camps."[12]

(During one of our later discussions about the situation in Chile during the military coup against Salvador Allende, Luis reminded me that during the Spanish Civil War, Pablo Neruda, the Chilean poet/diplomat and winner of the Nobel Prize for Literature in 1971, had organized a rescue ship to evacuate to Chile many Spanish socialists and intellectuals who feared for their lives at the hands of Franco's troops. Luis had a great admiration for the Chilean with whom he had dined on several occasions in Paris when Neruda was the Chilean ambassador to UNESCO.)

Of course, news of such ferocious reprisals against known socialists in Nationalist controlled territory in Spain resulted in a backlash in areas still under Republican control, with particular targets being the rich, bankers, landowners and especially the clergy, as the Church was seen to support the rebels. Given the number of extra-judicial murders and imprisonment of perceived left-wing supporters of the constitutional government one can understand the fears, not only of republican supporters but of the population in general – there were those who used the reprisals as an excuse to settle old scores. One example of the extremes to which individuals were prepared to go to avoid reprisals was the experience of Manuel Cortés, the last Republican mayor of the popular holiday resort of Mijas on the Costa del Sol in Andalucía, who fled from

---

[12] Paul Preston: The Spanish Holocaust, Prologue xi

his home when the Nationalists entered the village and only returned secretly after the war ended in 1939. However, such was his fear of being executed that he immediately went into hiding and did not feel it safe to reveal himself until the announcement of the amnesty for all civil war "offenders" in 1969 - thirty years later. Mijas today is a favourite holiday destination for British tourists and indeed many ex-pats have settled in the town. I suspect that not too many of them are aware of the story of Manuel Cortés.

At the university of Madrid during my first Spanish Literature class I was a bit surprised at how interested the professor was in my background. He questioned why I had not joined the classes conducted in English organised by one of the American Universities which had faculties in Madrid at the time. He eventually seemed satisfied when I explained that I had come to Spain to improve my Spanish and the last thing I wanted was to follow courses solely attended by English speakers. After the class I asked one of my Spanish friends whether the professor was always so inquisitive. "You have to understand, Eduardo, that it is the custom of the regime to keep tabs on the student population and to that end informers are often enrolled in classes. The prof was just testing you."

Whether that was the case or not I can't say but my friend seemed adamant that the practice was commonplace. What I can say with certainty is that there was considerable student unrest during my year at the university. Demonstrations against the regime were frequent and it was not uncommon to see police jeeps swing round the Arco de la Victoria - the 49m high arch constructed by Francisco Franco to celebrate his troops' victory in the 1936 'Battle of Ciudad Universitaria,' - and race towards the university, screeching to a halt before the protesting students. On one such occasion a police jeep pulled up in the road immediately beside the pavement where I was walking with other students on my return from classes in the Arts Faculty (Facultad de Filosofía y Letras.) The policemen who got out of the jeep seemed as apprehensive as I was. They had all the appearance of confused young lads who had just been brought in from the countryside, afraid to act without orders from the officer in charge. Fortunately, there was a ditch between the police and the pavement, and that hesitation allowed me to make my escape and take refuge in the Latin American Institute Library. On other occasions water-cannons were brought in to disperse the students and I remember asking one of my student friends why they took such risks with the police. "Every generation must do what it can to improve the political situation," he replied. Those words have stayed with me ever since, echoing as they did similar sentiments expressed by Robert Tressell in 1914:

"Every man who is not helping to bring about a better state of affairs for the future is helping to perpetuate the present misery and is therefore the enemy of his own children."[13]

Of course, away from the growing political unrest at the university, a pleasant walk through the Retiro Park, a stroll along the Castellana or enjoying *una caña* on the terrace of one of the bars in the Puerto del Sol, gave the impression of total freedom. Indeed, on the surface it would have appeared to the casual observer that Spaniards were reasonably sanguine about living in a dictatorship. In private, when they felt it safe to do

---

[13] Robert Tressell: The Ragged Trousered Philanthropists, p130

so, there were those who were prepared to criticise the regime but most just wanted to get on with their life without involving themselves in matters political which could cause problems for themselves or their families. One of my non-student friends, when asked about his attitude to the police, summed up in his broken-English what seemed to me to be the attitude of the general population, *"I don't bother them. They don't bother me."* As Marcuse so succinctly pointed out:

"The range of choice open to the individual is not the decisive factor in determining the degree of human freedom, but 'what' can be chosen and what 'is' chosen by the individual."[14]

The students understood this and reacted against anything designed to limit real choice. Two things in particular caught my attention during my stay. Firstly, there was the encouragement of sport by the regime, principally football and bullfighting, and secondly the constant reference to an external threat to the security of Spain - both designed to divert the attention of the populace from the political situation in the country. For this reason, many students disliked football which they saw as a way of diverting supporters' attention from the real problems facing Spain. They considered these diversions an obstacle to the political education of the people. Football, and not religion, was becoming the new opium of the masses. The fact that Real Madrid had won the European Cup five times in a row between 1956 and 1960 and again in season 1965/66, diverted the attention of many working people from what my student friends considered the more important social and economic problems which had such curtailing

---

[14] Herbert Marcuse: One Dimensional Man, p23

53

effect on the lives of ordinary citizens.

However, while the Madrid giants enjoyed the favour of the regime the same cannot be said about their great rivals, FC Barcelona. Historically the Catalan club had supported independence for Catalonia and this undoubtedly had provoked successive dictatorships. After General Primo de Rivera's coup d'état in 1923, restrictions were placed on FC Barcelona which included a ban on the use of the Catalan flag in the stadium, the registration with the police of all membership files, and the obligatory use of Castilian in the club's announcements. Things did not improve under Franco. On 6 August, 1936, the club's President, Josep Sunyol having left the town of Guadarrama, was travelling in a car flying the Catalan flag when he found himself on a stretch of road controlled not by militiamen from Madrid as he had expected but by Falangist troops loyal to the Nationalist rebellion. He was detained and subsequently executed. Between the end of the Civil War in 1939 and 1975 Franco's regime banned the use of Catalan in schools and in the public administration.

Fear has always been a weapon used in politics and the threat of an external enemy is a favourite ploy, principally, but not only of dictators. For the West it was the threat of Russia, then it was the Islamic State and terrorism and now we are warned that the major threat comes from China. For Franco and his co-conspirators, it was the threat of international communism, freemasonry and international Jewry. In 1967, believe it or not, the Spanish media was full of ominous warnings about the possibility of a major conflict with Britain over the disputed territory of Gibraltar. Tensions arose following the referendum in Gibraltar in which, of the 12,237 voters, only 44 voted in favour of Spanish sovereignty. The situation became so fraught that my wife wanted to catch the first flight home. Even some of my normally rational Spanish friends were becoming gung-ho. "Let them come", seemed to be the general attitude.

My wife had joined me in Madrid on Hogmanay, 31 December 1966. There we stayed in Calle Goya, a residential part of the city, with Dora (Adoración) and Avelino Arriola, the in-laws of my former landlady the widow of Avelino's brother. Dora was a lovely lady who would be about sixty years old and a devout Catholic, while Avelino, who appeared much older, and rather grumpy at times, certainly until he got to know us, declared himself to be a die-hard Republican. At first, they never talked about the civil war or the current political situation but after a while they felt confident enough to reveal something of their experiences of that time. We used to sit together of an evening during the winter around a circular table with a fitted ledge some twelve inches from the floor with a perfectly measured round hole which accommodated a circular electric fire which directed most of the heat towards the seats occupied by the old couple. "They're Scots. They don't feel the cold" I remember the old fellow say one particularly severe winter night as we sat in their freezing back kitchen with its stone floor and no central heating, and with my wife and I chilled to the marrow.

During these sessions Avelino would often return to his exploits as a loyal Republican and to his left-wing credentials – exploits which I took with a pinch of salt. He just didn't seem the type but perhaps I am doing him an injustice. Dora would warn him to keep his voice down. Even though we were sitting at the back of the house, in a kitchen with only a small window high up on the wall, and even though the war had ended thirty years previously, she still had a fear of being overheard. I was to experience a similar reluctance to speak openly about the Civil War a few years later in Santander where I was spending my summer holidays. There my wife and I befriended an old gentleman who had been in exile in America, having fled the country during the war, only returning when an amnesty was declared. His American pension allowed him to live in reasonable comfort now that he was back in Spain and he seemed to have settled happily back home. However, despite the passage of so many years, when I tried to engage him in discussions about his life during the Civil War, he became very uneasy and his voice dropped to a whisper. Recognising his discomfort, I dropped the subject. Memories of reprisals were obviously still vivid.

Despite her reluctance to engage in talk about politics and especially to be drawn into discussions about the war years, Dora was no shrinking violet. Indeed, she was an extremely courageous woman. She did admit to me on one occasion that she gave refuge to priests during the Republican backlash which followed news of Nationalist atrocities. I also got the impression that she shielded Republican sympathisers who were being hunted after the war. She was that kind of person – one of the most prejudice-free individuals I have ever met. She, as much as any person in my life, taught me a lot about tolerance.

Having studied the country's history and culture as I had, I was well aware of the situation in Spain during the Civil War and so I fully appreciated the difficulties the old couple would have faced during the war years. A good Spanish friend of my wife's uncle, whom I got to know really well over the years, was incarcerated after the war due to his Republican sympathies. He admitted to me that he was fortunate enough to be eventually released. Many thousands of Republican sympathisers were not so lucky. The very fact that a Republican flag hung on one of the walls in his house would have been enough to merit a prolonged jail sentence, if not worse, had it been discovered, but his wife covered it with a picture of the Virgen de Guadalupe – a seeming contradiction, but not unusual in Spain at the time. Just as was the case with Avelino and Dora here we had another Republican husband with a practising Catholic wife.

Links between Scotland and Spain

During my past research into links between Scotland and Spain I have spoken to one or two older relatives and friends who had either fought with the International Brigades or who had acquaintances who had done so. Others had participated in the many fund-raising concerts, fiestas and film shows organised by ordinary men and women in support of the beleaguered Spanish people. Their efforts were in stark contrast to the stance of the British government which had adopted a policy of non-intervention and of the official trade union movement which was reluctant to become involved due to the presence of communists in the aid programmes.

Over the years I have become increasingly aware of the many links between our two countries. Notable examples of these links include the sacrifice made by so many of the 549 Scots who left everything to enlist in the International Brigades formed to assist the Republican forces in their fight against fascism; the efforts of the Scottish Aid for Spain and the Spanish

Medical Programme; and the reception, 24 September 1937, at Montrose Park House in Montrose of 24 Basque children who fled Spain following the bombing of Guernica by the Luftwaffe. The heavy price paid by the volunteers at the Battles at Jarama, Brunete, Belchite and the Ebro, which was graphically described by some surviving 'brigadistas' in the TV documentary, "The Scots Who Fought Franco", narrated by David Hayman, was a stark reminder of the sacrifices Scots made in order to support the Spanish people. The International Brigade Memorial which can be seen on the Clyde Walkway at Customs House Quay, in Glasgow is another reminder of the close links between working people in both countries. Commissioned by the Glasgow Branch of the International Brigade Association, which raised the funds to finance Arthur Dooley's sculpture of Dolores Ibarruri, 'La Pasionaria', the Memorial was unveiled on 3 February, 1980 before a large crowd which was addressed by Jack Jones, a veteran of the International Brigade who went on to become General Secretary of the Transport and General Workers Union. The close ties which developed between the volunteers of the International Brigades and the Spanish people was illustrated by the thousands who lined the streets of Barcelona in September 1938 to bid farewell to the departing volunteers after the Republican Government announced the withdrawal of the International Brigades in the mistaken hope that Germany and Italy would reciprocate by withdrawing their forces. They left with the farewell address of 'La Pasionaria' ringing in their ears. Her impassioned address expressed the heartfelt gratitude of all Spanish Republicans, thousands of whom lined the streets of Barcelona to show their appreciation for the volunteers as they marched through the city on their way out of the country heading for neighbouring France and an unknown future. La Retirada, as the exodus came to be referred to by historians, saw nearly half a million civilians and soldiers cross the border, the single biggest influx of refugees ever known in France. The 'Reds' as they were dubbed were regarded as foreign undesirables which meant they could be legally imprisoned. About 60,000 men were placed in internment camps in Argelès-sur-Mer where they were housed in pitifully inadequate shacks with no water, no sanitation and little food.

Statue of La Pasionaria (Dolores Ibarruri) on the banks of the River Clyde opposite the Custom House, Clyde Street, Glasgow

Barcelona, November 1, 1938

"From all peoples, from all races, you came to us like brothers, like sons of immortal Spain; and in the hardest days of the war, when the capital of the Spanish Republic was threatened, it was you, gallant comrades of the International Brigades, who helped save the city with your fighting enthusiasm, your heroism and your spirit of sacrifice – And Jarama and Guadalajara, Brunete and Belchite, Levante and the Ebro, in immortal verses sing of the courage, the sacrifice, the daring, the discipline of the men of the International Brigades. For the first time in the history of the peoples' struggles, there was the spectacle, breath-taking in its grandeur, of the formation of International Brigades to help save a threatened country's freedom and independence – the freedom and independence of our Spanish land.

Communists, Socialists, Anarchists, Republicans – men of different colours, differing ideology, antagonistic religions – yet all profoundly loving liberty and justice, they came and offered themselves to us unconditionally. They gave us everything – their youth or their maturity; their science or their experience; their blood and their lives; their hope and aspirations – and they asked us for nothing. But yes, it must be said, they did want a post in battle, they aspired to the honour of dying for us. Banners of Spain! Salute these many heroes! Be lowered to honour so many martyrs!

Mothers! Women! When the years pass by and the wounds of war are staunched, when the memory of the sad and bloody days dissipates in a present of liberty, of peace and well-being; when the rancours have died out and pride in a free country is felt equally by all

Spaniards, speak to your children. Tell them of these men of the International Brigades.

Recount for them how, coming over seas and mountains, crossing frontiers bristling with bayonets, sought by ravenous dogs thirsting to tear their flesh, these men reached our country as crusaders for freedom, to fight and die for Spain's liberty and independence threatened by German and Italian fascism. They gave up everything – their loves, their countries, home and fortune, fathers, mothers, wives, brothers and sisters and children – and they came and said to us: "We are here. Your cause, Spain's cause, is ours. It is the cause of all advanced and progressive mankind.

Today many are departing. Thousands remain, shrouded in Spanish earth, profoundly remembered by all Spaniards. Comrades of the International Brigades: Political reasons, reasons of state, the welfare of that very cause for which you offered your blood with boundless generosity, are sending you back, some to your own countries and others to forced exile. You can go proudly. You are history. You are legend. You are the heroic example of democracy's solidarity and universality in the face of the vile and accommodating spirit of those who interpret democratic principles with their eyes on hoards of wealth or corporate shares which they want to safeguard from all risk. We shall not forget you, and, when the olive tree of peace is in flower, entwined with the victory laurels of the Republic of Spain – return! Return to our side for here you will find a homeland – those who have no country or friends, who must live deprived of friendship – all, all will have the affection and gratitude of the Spanish people who today and tomorrow will shout with enthusiasm -Long live the heroes of the International Brigades!

Not sentiments which will be shared by those who believe that democratically elected or not, Spain had to be saved from a left wing government, or those volunteers like the 700 Blue Shirts who sailed from Dun Laoghaire, County Dublin in Ireland with the blessing of the Church to support Franco's Nationalists and to prevent, as they believed, communism from gaining ground, but I make no apologies for including this full translation of Dolores Ibarruri's heartfelt thanks to the *brigadistas* from all parts of the globe who sacrificed everything to help the Spanish people. All of them, including the many Scots volunteers like Steve Fullarton, George Gowans, John Dunlop, John Londragan, Hugh Mackay and Jimmy Maley who figured in the aforementioned documentary deserve to be remembered. Their actions contrasted with the lack of response by the British government and the inertia of the official trade union movement to the threat to democracy posed by the rebel attack on the democratic government of Spain.

Chapter 6

Luis in Chile

"Whoever rises up and demands human and social advancement, which implies a reform of structures, let him prepare himself for slander campaigns, let him expect with certainty to be considered and opposed as a subversive and a communist."
Helder Camara, Archbishop of Olinda and Recife,
Brazil

In order to fully understand and appreciate the risks taken by Luis during his time in Santiago de Chile, it would be helpful to have some understanding of:

a) The history of democracy in Chile in the early part of the twentieth century up to the election of Salvador Allende's government in 1970,

b) The political situation in the country during Luis's time there, and

c) The involvement of the United States in Chilean politics.

The History of Democracy in Chile

During the period in question Chile was widely regarded as a beacon of democracy in Latin America, despite its many flaws and attempts to interfere in the democratic process by oligarchs and certain sections of the armed forces influenced covertly by the United States. After the de-facto dictatorship of General Carlos Ibañez, who held power in 1925 and from 1927 until constitutional government was restored in 1932, the Radical Party became the key force in coalition governments until 1952. Carlos Ibañez was then returned to office for a further six years before being succeeded, in 1958, by the conservative Jorge Alessandri.

The election in 1964 of the Christian Democratic Candidate for the presidency, Eduardo Frei Montalva, saw the introduction of major reforms in education, housing and agriculture. As is often the case with the best efforts of reformers, the reforms in question did not go far enough for left-wing groups and were considered excessive by conservative elements in the country. However, it was the result of the 1970 presidential election that set off a train of events which was to have a profound effect on Luis Ramallo's life in Santiago.

For the first time in Chile, and indeed in Latin America, a Marxist was democratically elected to the highest post in the land. In a three-way contest Senator Salvador Allende Gossens, a member of the Socialist Party who headed the Popular Unity coalition of broadly left-wing parties, received 36% of the votes while the former conservative President Alessandri received 35% and Radomiro Tomic of the Christian Democratic Party 28%. In a run-off vote, influenced by the murder of the constitutionalist Commander-in-chief of the armed forces, General Rene Schneider and the refusal of the Christian Democrats to back Allessandri, Allende received 153 votes to Allessandri's 35.

Politics in Chile During Luis's Tenure of Office at Flacso

The election of Allende to the presidency coincided

64

with Luis's tenure as the fourth and last director of ELAS, The Latin American School of Sociology in Santiago. ELAS was part of the FLACSO project (The Latin American Faculty of Social Sciences) which was created in 1957 with the support of UNESCO, the Chilean government, the University of Chile, and with the contributions of those governments in Latin America which signed up to the project. The fate of Allende and the ELAS programme would be inextricably linked.

Once in office Allende pursued a programme of political reforms which he referred to as "The Chilean Way to Socialism", a road which he insisted would be democratic, legal and peaceful. His programme included the nationalisation of the copper mines, the health care system and the coal mines, and a programme of free milk for children. He also continued his predecessor Frei's education policies and the process of land distribution that had occurred from 1962 to 1973 with the initial support of most political parties and the Church.

The previous government of Eduardo Frei had already partly nationalised the copper industry by acquiring a 51% share in foreign owned mines. However, Allende's plan was to fully nationalise foreign mines. Although the Chilean constitution called for just compensation according to "minimal international standards", by means of a series of deductions for "loans invested poorly" and "excessive profits" going back twenty years, compensation to three of the five foreign companies was eliminated.

Allende's clear aim was to improve the lot of the poorest sectors of Chilean society and to this end he provided employment in new nationalised projects or on public works. Salaries and wages were increased, taxes were reduced, and pensions were increased for widows, invalids, orphans and the elderly. A National Milk Plan was introduced which provided for half a litre of milk, free of charge, to almost three and a half million children and the land-redistribution reforms initiated by the previous president, Eduardo Frei, proceeded apace.

However, rising food prices negated the improvement in the income of the workers. Initial industrial growth soon contracted, the government deficit soared at an alarming rate due to the fall in copper prices, lack of economic aid and strikes by lorry drivers all combined to negate efforts to improve the economic and social well-being of the Chilean poor. Divisions in the ruling Unidad Popular government and even within Allende's own Socialist Party added to the chaos.

U.S Involvement in Chile

Given the U.S. distaste for the socialist policies being introduced by the Chilean government, fear of the effect the example of another socialist run country would have on other countries in the region and antagonism towards the socialist government in Cuba in particular, it was certainly a mistake by Allende to invite Fidel Castro to Chile in 1972 and to extend his stay to three weeks. The Monroe Doctrine as expressed by President James Monroe in 1823 was originally meant as a warning to European powers that the US would resist, militarily if necessary, any attempt by European powers to colonize the Americas but it has cast a long shadow over US foreign policy ever since its introduction. The Americas are still regarded in the U.S. as America's sphere of influence.

The U.S. had actively sought to block Allende's route to the Presidency. The CIA had covertly spent three million dollars campaigning against him, mainly through the media, backing Eduardo Frei Montalva of the Christian Democratic Party. America not only directly contributed $20 million to the campaign but sent in about 100 people to try to thwart an Allende victory. If that failed the CIA had a plan B which involved seeking out and supporting military officers who might be willing to back a coup d'état. The murder of the constitutionalist General Rene Schneider, who was seen as an obstacle to this plan, was covered up by the CIA and the White House.

The scene was set for the inevitable outcome to this U.S. involvement in a regime change which followed to the letter the three-stage process for regime change described by Stephen Kinzer in his book *Overthrow* and quoted in Naomi Klein's *The Shock Doctrine*. First a U.S. based multinational corporation faces a threat to its bottom line by the actions of a foreign government, in this case the nationalisation of the Kennecott and Anaconda Copper Corporation's mines in Chile. Second this action is interpreted by U.S. Politicians as an attack on the U.S. Third, the politicians have to convince the public of the need for intervention. People must be convinced that what is involved here is a struggle between good and evil, a struggle to free a poor downtrodden people from the grip of a corrupt government or dictator.

Preparations for a Coup

"We'll make the economy scream"
President Richard Nixon

Having failed to stop Allende's election to the Presidency, the Nixon government covertly embarked on a series of measures designed to undermine his authority and destabilise the economy - "We'll make the economy scream." Following a report from the CIA station in Santiago, the organisation responsible for covert operations, which was headed by Henry Kissinger, approved a request for one million dollars to support "opposition parties and private sector organisations," including support for the strike of lorry drivers which was crippling the economy. There was to be no let-up in the Dirty War against a socialist government which, it was feared, was going down the Cuban route.

Emboldened by US opposition to Allende's government and previous contacts regarding possible support for military intervention by the Chilean army, on 29 June 1973 there was an attempted coup led by Lieutenant Colonel Roberto Souper against the elected Government. The coup, "El Tancazo" - so-called because the officers involved relied primarily on the use of tanks - was put down by loyal troops led by the army Commander-in-Chief, General Carlos Prats, who also served in the Allende Government as Minister of Defence.

However, the failed coup was a mere prelude to what was to follow. The position of General Prats, whose loyal forces had so successfully put down the attempted coup, became increasingly untenable as the weeks passed. A vociferous demonstration outside the General's house on 21 August by the wives of military officers, angry at what they considered his total support for Allende, was an indication of the continuing and growing opposition among middle and upper-class Chileans to government policies.

Demonstrations by military wives was bad enough but it was clear to Prats that they had the support of their husbands. Indeed, he had witnessed the presence of some officers at the demonstration.

Refusal to sign a pledge of loyalty by most of the generals as demanded by Prats forced the General to consider his own position. He could resign and hope that his likely replacement, General Augusto Pinochet, could dissuade the Army from embarking on a treasonous course of action or he could risk civil war by forcing the resignation of a dozen or so of the most rebellious generals. A sick man, he had no stomach for the latter course of action. He did not want the blood of his fellow countrymen and women on his hands and so, at a meeting with President Allende, 23 August, he offered his resignation and, ironically, recommended Augusto Pinochet as his successor:

"President, if you nominate General Pinochet, who has so often given me proof of his loyalty, there is still the possibility of calming the situation. That would give you time to come to an agreement with the Christian Democrats. And Pinochet could send the two or three most troublesome generals into retirement."[15]

Given the horrors which were to befall the Chilean people, or at least to those who supported, or were suspected of supporting the Popular Unity Government, Prats' endorsement of his friend Pinochet was rather ironic, not least because of his ultimate reward for that endorsement. However, given such a recommendation, his own observations of Pinochet's loyalty and reports from others inside his government, Allende appointed Pinochet to succeed Prats as Commander-in-Chief of the Army on 23 August 1973.

---

[15] Ernesto Ekaizer: Yo, Augusto, p48

Raymond Warren, Head of the CIA delegation at the American Embassy in Santiago, was in constant contact with CIA Headquarters in Langley, Virginia, keeping those responsible for covert operations, including Henry Kissinger, up to date with events in Chile. The resignation of the constitutionalist General Prats, Minister of Defence and Commander-in-chief of the Army, and his replacement by Augusto Pinochet as Commander-in-Chief and by Orlando Letelier as Defence Minister, were reported back to Langley almost as soon as the changes were announced. Indeed, on 8 September, three days before the coup took place, full details of the plan of action and the names of the major conspirators were communicated to Langley in a full report from Warren. "So, there's going to be a coup in Chile," observed Kissinger, as if that would have come as a surprise. In fact, Langley knew the exact details of the timing of the coup on 10 September, the day before the coup was to take place, when the covert operations team received the following coded communique:

"An attempted coup will begin 11 September. The three branches of the Armed Forces and the Police are taking part in this action. A declaration will be read at 7 a.m. 11 September. The Police will be responsible for arresting the President, Salvador Allende.[16]

Up until a couple of days before the coup, Pinochet's participation in the rebellion was not certain. His position from the outset was rather ambiguous. Regarded by his friend Prats and even by Allende himself as being loyal to the government, he was not altogether trusted by the conspirators who were unsure as to the position he would adopt when the

---

[16] Ernesto Ekaizer: Yo, Augusto, p97

coup eventually took place. The plans for unseating Allende and replacing the Popular Unity government with a Military Junta was being driven from Valparaiso by the Navy and Air Force. It was only on Sunday 9 September that he finally signed up to the conspiracy and so when the coup came, on the morning of 11 September, it was supported by all sections of the armed forces, Army, Navy and Air Force, as well as the national police force (the Carabineros). The three-year experience of the first democratically elected socialist government was all but over and what was to follow echoed the worst atrocities of the Spanish Civil War.

Allende's Final Address to the Nation

Once the bombs began to fall and reports came in to the Moneda Palace of troop movements and the cancelling of all leave at the Santiago barracks, Allende decided that it was time to speak to the Chilean people about the situation before all means of communication were cut off. The following is a translation of that speech:

"This will surely be my last opportunity to address you. The Air Force has bombed the towers of Radio Portales and Radio Corporación. My words have no bitterness but rather disappointment. Let them be a moral punishment for those who have betrayed their oath: Soldiers of Chile, titular commanders-in-chief, Admiral Merin - who has designated himself Commander of the Navy - and Señor Mendoza, the despicable general who only yesterday was pledging his fidelity and loyalty to the Government, and who has also appointed himself Chief of the National Police Force.

71

Faced with these facts, the only thing left for me is to tell the workers that 'I am not going to resign.' Placed in a historic transition, I will repay the people's loyalty with my life. And I say to you that I am certain that the seed we have sown in the dignified conscience of thousands and thousands of Chileans will not be forever withered.

Workers of my country: I want to thank you for the loyalty that you have always shown, the confidence that you deposited in a man who was no more than the interpreter of great yearnings for justice, a man who gave his word that he would respect the Constitution and the Law and who did just that. At this definitive moment, the last moment I have to address you, I wish you to learn from this lesson: foreign capital, imperialism, together with internal reaction, created the climate in which the Armed Forces broke with their tradition, the tradition taught by General Schneider and reaffirmed by Commander Araya, victims of the same social sector which will today be in their homes hoping, with foreign assistance, to retake power to continue defending their profits and their privileges.

I especially address the modest women of our land, the peasant farmer who believed in us, the worker who worked harder, the mother who knew our concern for their children. I address the professionals of our country, patriotic professionals, those who a few days ago continued to work against the sedition sponsored by professional associations, class-based associations that also defended the advantages which a capitalist society grants to a few. I address the youth, those who sang and gave us their joy and their spirit of struggle. I address the man of Chile, the worker, the farmer, the intellectual, those who will be persecuted, because in our country fascism has already been present for many hours: in terrorist attacks, blowing up bridges, cutting rail-road tracks, destroying the oil and gas pipelines, in the face of those who had an obligation to defend them.

No doubt Radio Magallanes will be silenced, and the calm metal of my voice will no longer reach you. It does not matter. You will continue to hear it. I will always be near you. At least my memory will be that of a man of dignity who was loyal to the loyalty of the workers. The people must defend themselves, but they must not sacrifice themselves. They must not let themselves be destroyed or riddled with bullets, but they must not be humiliated either.

Workers of my country, I have faith in Chile and its destiny. Other men will overcome this grey and bitter moment when treason seeks to prevail. Go forward knowing that sooner rather than later, the great avenues will open again, where free men will walk to build a better society. Long live Chile! Long live the people! Long live the workers!

These have been my last words, and I am certain that my sacrifice will not be in vain. I am certain that, at the very least, it will be a moral lesson that will punish felony, cowardice and treason."[17]

After his broadcast Allende gathered together all those members of his administrative staff, advisers and bodyguards who were still in the Moneda and advised all non-essential people to leave the Palace while there was still time.

---

[17] Ernest Ekaizer: Yo, Augusto, pp115/116

Chapter 7

The Bloody Aftermath

"Why didn't they talk in their first interrogation and save themselves all that pointless suffering? In the end they either confessed or they died, like this fellow they were getting ready for execution."

Of Love and Shadows: Isabel Allende

Once the bombardment of La Moneda was over and the troops had taken the building, Pinochet's orders, that there was to be no softly, softly approach to any opposition, meant that the terror that was to last for years afterwards began in earnest. Allende had committed suicide and his advisers and officials had been rounded up. The full horror of what followed is graphically described by Ernesto Ekaizer in his thoroughly researched account of the fate which befell those Allende supporters:

On the night of 11/12, officers of the Military Intelligence Service (SIM) interrogated them under torture. They were informed that they would be shot that very day, at mid-night; later they were told that the execution would take place at 3 a.m. and a little later that it would be 6 a.m. Finally, Colonel Joaquín Ramírez Pineda, in contact with Major Pedro Espinoza, member of SIM and commander of the army in Santiago, at 12 mid-day ordered Second Lieutenant Jorge Ivan Herrera to transfer the 21 prisoners to Peldehue where the Tacna Regiment carried out military manoeuvres ....twenty kilometres from Santiago. One by one the prisoners, bound hand and foot with galvanised wire, were identified by an officer in plain clothes as they climbed into a Pegaso military lorry.

Colonel Ramírez Pineda ordered First Lieutenant Juan Riquelme to bring a box of ten or fifteen grenades to be used in the mission..........Once in Peldehue, Major Pedro Espinoza took charge of the operation. A machine-gun was placed on the ground a short distance from a well which would have been about fifteen metres deep. The detainees got down from the lorry one by one. They were placed in front of the well with their back to the machine-gun. Second Lieutenant Herrera fired the shots. Before leaving, the officers who supervised the operation threw the grenades into the well.

An officer wearing a uniform which showed no rank lined up the Tacna soldiers, 'What you have seen and heard never happened, remember it well. Everything was done for the Fatherland. These Marxists deserved to die. Now you will all return to your unit.'

The language used echoed the conversations General Pinochet had with Admiral Patrício Carvajal and General Leigh hours before the bombardment of the Moneda Palace.

Back with the regiment Colonel Ramirez Pineda assembled the fourteen soldiers who had taken part in the mission and told them: "This is what had to be done with these people, all dangerous Marxists. Nothing will happen to you because they were condemned at a summary trial by a military tribunal. Don't worry."[18]

In the meantime, the operation to round up left-wing activists and anyone suspected of supporting the

---

[18] Ernesto Ekaizer: Yo, Augusto, pp151/152

Popular Unity government was well under way. According to a report by Amnesty International up to 7,000 political prisoners were being held in the Chile Stadium on 22 September 1973, eleven days after the coup. The stadium became a concentration camp where, together with many other sites in Santiago, many political activists were interrogated and tortured before eventually being murdered. This was to become the norm in Pinochet's Chile.

Among the many who suffered in the stadium, one of the most famous, certainly among the young people, was Victor Lidio Jara Martínez, teacher, poet, singer-songwriter and committed supporter of the Allende Government. Jara was among the first to be arrested after the coup and interned in the Estadio Chile along with university students, professors, workers and others. There he was tortured and his hands and fingers smashed by guards who proceeded to taunt him, inviting him to play his guitar for his *compañeros.* His subsequent murder was described by the Brazilian journalist, Mauricio Brum, in his book "Estadio Chile, 1973", in which he quotes Brazilian detainee, Pedro Enrique Wrede who witnessed Jara's final moments:

"The death occurred between 15/16 September. The soldiers were amusing themselves playing Russian-roulette and killed Victor Jara. Afterwards they fired forty shots into the body to make it look like he was killed in an exchange of gunfire."

Following his death Jara's body was left at the entrance of the stadium for the other prisoners to see before being unceremoniously dumped in some back street of the capital. Like that of so many other anonymous civilian victims of the Chilean Army, whether murdered or who simply disappeared, Victor Jara's fate was but a statistic to the Generals. The details of his torture and death were revealed by a Truth and Reconciliation Commission created in 1990, two years after the Chilean National Plebiscite, 5 October 1988, in which the majority of Chileans voted against extending Pinochet's rule for another eight years, thus bringing to an end sixteen years of military dictatorship. However, it was not until July 2018 that eight military officers were sentenced to fifteen years each for Victor Jara's murder. (See Appendix B)

Given the sheer number of prisoners held in the stadium and the number of soldiers required to guard them there was no way that the horror of what occurred there could be kept secret and rumours about torture and executions quickly began to circulate. However, it was not until June 2000 that an army guard, on duty in the stadium at the time, confirmed on state television the full horrors of the events he witnessed. Roberto Saldías, a non-commissioned officer, stated on national television that he had witnessed people being taken away for execution. When prisoners entered the stadium, they were placed in groups which were identified by yellow, black or red discs. Those unfortunate enough to be identified by a red disc in the words of Saldías "had no chance." They were marked for execution. His testimony was particularly important as for the first time a member of the military was prepared to forego anonymity and to speak openly about what he had witnessed. He identified Lieutenant Armando Fernández Larios as being particularly brutal and sadistic labelling him "the biggest murderer in Chile. He is a psychopath and murderer." Larios fled to the United States in the late 1970s.

Documents referring to human-rights abuses during the Pinochet dictatorship which were declassified on the orders of President Clinton and made public in July

2000, contained information about the murder of three United States citizens killed in the aftermath of the coup. Frank R. Terrugi Jr. was a student who had been on an FBI surveillance list due to what was regarded as 'socialist' sympathies. He was arrested at his apartment, taken to the National Stadium, tortured and executed. His bullet-riddled body was found in the morgue a few days later. Charles Horman was an American journalist who was murdered in the National Stadium 19 September 1973 and his body dumped on the streets. His story was the subject of the 1982 film, 'Missing', directed by Costa-Gavras and starring Jack Lemmon. Boris Weisfeller was a mathematics professor who was picked up by the military while hiking in Chile in 1985. According to his sister Olga, the documents indicated that he had been tortured and killed in a secret concentration camp. A statement released in a memo from the U.S. State Department revealed that during the coup U.S. intelligence "may have played an unfortunate part in the killings of two American citizens, Charles Horman and Frank Terrugi Jr. At best, it was limited to providing or confirming information that helped motivate murder by the government of Chile."

In 2011 Chilean judge Jorge Zepeda issued a criminal indictment for the murders of Horman and Terrugi against former U.S. military official, Captain Ray E. Davis and former Chilean army colonel, Pedro Espinoza, who was already serving time for human-rights offences in Chile and who as a member of the Military Intelligence Service (SIM) has already been referred to as having played a major part in the execution of Allende's advisers on 12 September 1973. In June 2013 Judge Zepeda ruled that Davis, who had been in charge of the U.S. Military Group in Chile and who had had a personal encounter with Horman just days before his execution, had in fact participated in Horman's murder as well as that of Terrugi.

Of course, the carnage wreaked by the Chilean Army was not restricted to the capital, nor was it short-lived. Pinochet designated General Sergio Arellano Stark "Official Delegate" of the President of the Military Junta, with authority over the Commanders-in-Chief of the provinces he visited. His orders were to accelerate the detention of political prisoners and to ensure there was uniformity of purpose among regional commanders. His mission, as he moved from city to city in search of dissidents, became known as the "Caravan of Death" in that it resulted in the imprisonment, torture and summary execution of prisoners, often without even the fig-leaf of a trial by Court Martial, and often after having had decisions of local commanders overruled.

According to the National Commission on Political Imprisonment and Torture (Valech Report), prepared at the request of President Ricardo Lagos, which met between September 2003 and June 1, 2005, and the Commission of Truth and Reconciliation (Rettig Report, 1991) there were approximately 30,000 victims of human rights abuses in Chile during Pinochet's rule, including 27,255 tortured and 2,279 executed. Of course these statistics would include dissidents who were victims of *Operation Condor*, a U.S backed campaign of political repression and state terror which was inaugurated in Santiago de Chile on 25 November 1975 at a meeting chaired by Manuel Contreras, head of the Chilean Secret Service (DINA), and attended by representatives of the secret services of the dictatorships in Argentina, Bolivia, Brazil, Paraguay and Uruguay – such were the paragons of democracy who were Nixon and Kissinger's bed-fellows.

Augusto Pinochet   Pinochet (left) embraces
greets Henry Kissinger   Sergio Arellano

The Plan was that there should be cross border liaison between the various services in the clandestine persecution of left-wing militants, trade unionists, students, and intellectuals and to coordinate any actions against them, including repression, torture, murder and disappearance.

U.S. Army and CIA interrogation manuals, which incorporated material from CIA and Army manuals written in the 1950's and 1960's and used between 1987 and 1991 for training courses at the U.S. Army *School of the Americas,* were declassified by the Pentagon in 1996. The two CIA manuals, referred to as the 'torture manuals', which were declassified following a Freedom of Information Act request by the Baltimore Sun, explain better than any words of mine just what ongoing U.S. involvement in Latin America meant to the people of that region. (See Appendex A) The release of these manuals which advocated torture, extortion, blackmail and the targeting of civilian populations, proved what human rights organisations had been saying all along, namely that U.S. taxpayers had been funding the teaching of torture and repression.

The fact that the writ of *Operación Condor* extended far beyond the borders of Pinochet's Chile meant that no one was safe even if they managed to escape the country. General Carlos Prats González, former Commander-in-Chief of the Chilean Army and Pinochet's predecessor, did not escape the attention of the DINA. He had been granted safe conduct out of the country although not before being forced to give a public assurance that he would not conspire against the Junta while in exile. Not that the assurance guaranteed his safety. Along with his wife he was killed by a car bomb outside his apartment in Buenos Aires on 30 September 1974. Another high-profile victim of Operation Condor was Chilean ambassador Orlando Letelier, a former minister in Allende's Government, who was also killed by a car bomb in Washington in 1976.

These were the people in control of Chile during the time my good friend Luis Ignacio Ramallo Massanet worked for Unesco in Santiago de Chile. The unassuming old gentleman who can often be found of an evening sitting in a quiet corner of the "Restaurante Cala Canta" in Ciutat Jardi in Mallorca, quietly reading his book, has many a tale to tell. Not that he would ever initiate a conversation about what he has witnessed and experienced during the time he was contracted to work with UNESCO in Chile. His actions during this turbulent period in Chilean history demonstrate the risks many ordinary citizens are prepared to take, and the lengths to which they are often prepared to go, in order to give succour to fellow human beings in danger of being tortured or indeed murdered.

Chapter 8

Death, Torture or Exile

"Any man's death diminishes me, because I am involved in Mankind"
John Donne

As Director of ELAS (the Latin American School of Sociology), attached to Flacso (Latin American Faculty of Social Sciences), at the University of Chile, Luis Ramallo was confronted with the fact that the whereabouts and safety of up to forty of his students and colleagues was a cause for considerable concern during the days following the coup d'état. Some had been picked up by the military and were being held in the National Stadium while others were in hiding, fearful for their safety. Indeed, one of Luis's colleagues Doctor Jorge Klein, who was married to the sister of Luis's deputy, Ayrton Fausto, was among the twenty-one prisoners taken from La Moneda on 11 September and executed the following day. Klein, besides being a colleague and a doctor, was also considered by Luis to be one of his best students – he was taking a post-graduate course in sociology. As a member of the Socialist Party Jorge Klein, apart from being one of Allende's personal physicians, was part of the close group, including a number of Cubans, who were detailed to protect the President. He was one of the few people who had remained at Allende's side even when the President urged everyone to leave once it became clear that all was lost. He was still at his side when the President took his own life. Jorge Klein paid the ultimate price for his loyalty to Allende and his death, along with that of the others who had been rounded up with him following Allende's suicide, alerted Luis and others to the immediate danger to other colleagues and students.

José Serra

"No one can help everyone, but everyone can help someone"
> Anon

Fortunately, due to the coordinated efforts of a group of people from Flacso including Luis, José Serra and Ricardo Lagos Escobar, many of those who considered themselves to be in immediate danger were able to find refuge in Flacso Headquarters or school buildings. As recounted to me by Luis and verified by the testimony of Ricardo Lagos Escobar, the Chilean lawyer, economist and teacher at the University of Santiago, who became President of Chile between 2000 and 2006, the case of José Serra was particularly interesting in that it demonstrated the risks taken by many individuals who were prepared to put their freedom, if not their lives, on the line in order to save others at a time when summary executions were not uncommon.

Serra was a Brazilian national who, as President of the National Union of Students, was sentenced to imprisonment in Brazil after the military coup which ousted President Goulart in 1964. He took refuge in the Bolivian Embassy in Rio de Janeiro where he spent three months before going into exile, first in France and then in Chile. There he became a member of the Latin American Faculty of Social Sciences, which was sponsored by the UN, teaching economics at the University of Chile. He also became one of President Allende's economic advisers.

After the military coup in Chile, Serra used his influence as a functionary of FLACSO to assist the escape of other wanted foreigners who were living in Chile. With Luis, Lagos Escobar and others, he was part of a group which undertook to find ways to help several people escape the country or find safe haven within FLACSO premises. However, their efforts were often thwarted by the vigilance of the military who very quickly took control of the international airport and the border points near Santiago.

Unfortunately for Serra his name figured on a Ministry of Foreign Affairs document which sought information on foreigners living in Chile. Shortly after the coup Luis was working with other professors and teachers, including Serra and Ricardo Lagos, in his office at Flacso Headquarters, 51 José Miguel Infante Street in Santiago, correcting work which had been submitted by students, when the terrified janitor of the building came running upstairs to announce that armed soldiers in full battle dress had burst into the building. Luis was furious.

Accompanied by Alain Touraine, an eminent French sociologist whom Luis described as a brilliant scholar, one of the best sociologists in the world, and his deputy Ayrton Fausto, he ran downstairs to confront the intruders. "I didn't know if I would even reach the bottom of the stairs," he admitted. "But I was younger then and impetuous and never thought about what I was doing or the danger I might be putting myself in by confronting armed soldiers." He demanded to know who was in charge and by what, or whose, authority they had dared to enter the building.

They were looking for José Serra. "José Serra is upstairs, but this is not his residence. This is a U.N. building. José works for the U.N. and I am the Secretary General of the U.N. in this building. You cannot touch him. You have no authority here so get out." The soldiers left but only to station themselves across the street from the Flacso Headquarters. Fortunately, working upstairs in Luis's office was a former Deputy Minister of Foreign Affairs in Chile who was still loyal to Allende and who was beginning to get involved with the group endeavouring to find safe places for those in possible danger. He made a call to the Minister of Foreign Affairs who, although a very well-known member of the army, was not a supporter of Pinochet and had not taken part in the coup. As a result of that call there was a communication from the Ministry to the soldiers outside which led to them departing the scene.

Following this confrontation with the military Luis determined to embark on two specific courses of action. Firstly, in talks with the government he insisted that the Ministry of Foreign Relations put into writing Law 17.328 of 26 August 1970, and article X1, paragraph 1 of the Paris agreement between the Chilean Government and the United Nations. The agreements included in these documents recognised the inviolability (immunity from raids) of Flacso premises and their immunity from jurisdiction. This was agreed by the Ministry and a notice to this effect, signed by Luis as the Responsible Functionary of FLACSO and Nicanor Díaz Estrada on behalf of the Ministry for Foreign Relations, was posted not only in FLACSO headquarters but in other UN agencies.

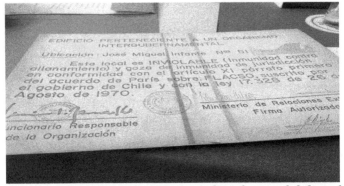

The agreement signed by Luis recording the inviolability of the FLACSO building at 51 José Miguel Infante Street in Santiago, Chile

His second, and even more pressing course of action, was to quickly find a solution to the ongoing problem of Serra's safety. Despite the agreement regarding the inviolability of FLACSO premises Luis was not entirely convinced that this would always be respected by the Junta, and of course Serra could not safely leave the premises. One possible solution discussed by the group was to go down the Joan Garcés route. (He, Garcés, was secretly lodged in the Spanish embassy until he could eventually be flown out of the country to safety.) Serra, although a Brazilian national, had Italian grandparents. A call was made to the Italian Embassy. Unfortunately, the Ambassador was out of the country but the functionary in charge in his absence was sympathetic and agreed that Serra could be given asylum in the Embassy. He was taken there by Luis and his deputy, Ayrton Fausto. The hope was that, after a short stay, he would receive an Italian passport which would allow him to leave Chile. However, as it transpired his stay in the Embassy was not a short one and his exit from Chile was not to be easily achieved.

On 14 October 1973, just over a month after the coup, with papers prepared by the Italian Embassy, Serra, accompanied by Luis and a secretary from the embassy, was driven to the airport to catch a 'plane out of the country. Initially everything seemed to be going well. Luis was greeted cordially by the commandant in charge who remembered him from his previous involvement with Garcés and three other Spaniards who had been allowed to leave the country. Serra was able to board the plane unimpeded. However, Luis's relief was short-lived. Shortly after boarding the Brazilian was brought back out of the plane and escorted to the commandant's office. The officer insisted that Serra's papers were not in order and he was informed that he would be taken back into the city to Police Headquarters. Once there, Serra and Luis insisted that as an official of FLACSO the Brazilian enjoyed diplomatic immunity. Luis refused to leave the building until the matter was resolved. It was then decided that Serra would be taken from Police Headquarters to the National Stadium where political prisoners were being held. Luis then insisted on accompanying him there and followed in his official car. He was only too well aware that the men escorting Serra to the stadium had no great regard for FLACSO. The Brazilian, as a friend and adviser to Allende, figured high on the list of most wanted foreigners and after what had happened to Jorge Klein and others the morning after the coup Luis determined to ensure that Serra was indeed taken to the stadium.

According to the Chilean Journalist, Mauricio Weiber, secret documents which he researched for his book "Associaçao Ilícita", include the document which saved Serra's life – it was a letter sent by the General Secretary of FLACSO, Luis Ramallo, which demanded the Ministry of Foreign Affairs release Serra who, it stressed, enjoyed immunity as a functionary of an institution sponsored by the UN. Indeed, when the Italian ambassador returned, he accompanied Luis to the National Stadium where Serra was released into the custody of the Ambassador. For the next year he remained in exile in the Italian Embassy until he was finally given an Italian passport and allowed to leave Chile. His later political career in Brazil included a stint as Sao Paulo's State Secretary of Economics and Planning, election as Senator for the State of Sao Paulo, and an unsuccessful attempt to become President of Brazil. On 12 May 2016, he became Minister of Foreign affairs in the government of President Michel Temer.

Joan Garcés

Cast a cold eye on life, on death. Horseman pass by!
W.B. Yeats

Another of Luis's successful interventions on behalf of fugitives from the military concerned another of Allende's advisers, Joan Garcés. Born in Valencia, Spain, Garcés worked for the United Nations - specifically UNESCO - and taught at the Latin American School of Political Sciences and Public Administration. He was contracted by Allende as adviser in 1970. When it was clear, 11 September, that all was lost and that La Moneda Palace was about to be taken by the military, Allende took Garcés aside and advised him to leave. When the Spaniard protested that he preferred to stay with the others he was reminded by the President that someone had to survive to give the Government's version of events and to challenge that of the "golpistas." He was to be that someone and the man who would come back to haunt Pinochet decades later.

What followed was described in great detail by Ernesto Ekaizer and confirmed to me by Luis. Once outside the palace, Garcés made his way to the flat of his brother Vincent's friend, Joaquín Leguina, a Spanish demographer who had been contracted by the Latin American Centre of Demography in March 1973. There he was joined by the Catalan town planner Jordi Borja and his wife Carmen Guinea a teacher at a primary school for blind children in Barcelona. As Garcés's name figured prominently on the list of wanted people which appeared on the military edict which was read out on radio and television stations, Borja, recognising the immediacy of the danger to Garcés, insisted that it was imperative to find a way to smuggle him out of the country and to safety as soon as possible. He phoned Luis to discuss how best this could be done.

Luis immediately contacted Enrique Iglesias who, as Executive Secretary of the Economic Commission for Latin America, was the man responsible for the security and well-being of all UN personnel in times of crisis. They agreed to meet at the headquarters of CEPAL, the UN Economic Commission for Latin America and the Caribbean. There Luis explained the imminent danger to Garcés and the need to devise a plan to guarantee his safety. Fearing that the Chilean military might possibly disregard UN immunity, Iglesias's first suggestion was to find him refuge in some Latin American embassy which could invoke an asylum agreement. On second thoughts, however, he suggested it might be better to put the matter into the hands of the Spanish ambassador and that Luis should be the one to explain the situation to him. Iglesias arranged the meeting.

When Luis laid the facts before him, the ambassador, Enrique Pérez-Hernández, gave the matter some thought before commenting that, if the UN wasn't thought to be protection enough, it was entirely possible that the Spanish embassy wouldn't be able to provide the necessary protection either. *"I know something about the military mentality, Ramallito. I was in the Spanish Civil War with Franco and I'm telling you Chilean military men are much more brutal than ours".* [19] The ambassador suggested that Luis leave the matter in his hands and that he should contact him later in the day. He advised Luis that, in the meantime, he must exercise extreme caution when communicating with him. Luis remembers well the ambassador's parting words to him, *"Si te queda algo de orgullo español, ésta es la hora de demostrarlo."* Back at his office in FLACSO, Luis used a secure line to inform Enrique Iglesias that the matter was now in the hands of the Spanish Ambassador.

Iglesias went to the Ministry of Defence on 14 September where he discussed the Garcés case with the Minister, Huerta, who insisted that the Spaniard was guilty of serious crimes and had to be tried. Since Garcés's name was obviously high on the list of wanted men, Iglesias came away from the meeting with the clear impression that there was every possibility that the Junta would ignore UN immunity in this case. If Garcés's life was to be saved they would have to act quickly. He went immediately to the Spanish ambassador's house to explain the need for urgency. It was agreed that Garcés should be brought to the

---

[19] Ernesto Ekaiser: Yo, Augusto, p150

ambassador's house without delay.

As Luis explained to me during our conversations about his time in Chile, his official car had UN number plates which permitted him to move freely about the city even during curfew hours. This allowed him to take Garcés safely to the ambassador's house, despite the obvious danger to himself as well as to his companion. When Garcés gave him the keys to his house and asked him to pick up some incriminating papers Luis assumed the responsibility despite the further danger to his own safety, another example of what ordinary people are prepared to do *in extremis*. Back at FLACSO Luis called the ambassador to inform him that he had taken Garcés to his home.

Later the ambassador had the Spaniard's brother Vincent brought to the house too and there they were joined by two others, the engineer Ernesto Torrealba, a member of the Socialist Party, and a Spaniard whose identity has never been revealed, although Ernesto Ekaizer hints that he was a person of interest to General Franco. The ambassador, at a meeting with Pinochet, 17 September, succeeded in persuading the General to approve the granting of four safe conducts for his guests. Joan Garcés, his brother Vicente, Ernesto Torrealba and the mystery fourth political refugee flew out of Chile, Saturday 22 September, on the Spantax 'plane which had brought in medical supplies that same day. Little did Pinochet realise that Joan Garcés would come back to haunt him 25 years later.

While negotiations for the safe conduct of these four fortunate individuals were proceeding, and arrangements were being made for their subsequent departure from Chile, the roundup of perceived opponents of the regime was gathering momentum.

The Fate of an Unidentified Bolivian Student

In history, the man in the ruffled shirt and gold-laced waistcoat somehow levitates above the blood he has ordered to be spilled by dirty-handed underlings.

Francis Jennings

Of course, it was not just Luis's colleagues who were in fear of their lives. Many of his students were too. During our many conversations he often referred to the occasions when he was required to go with his credentials to the National Stadium or to city morgues in order to identify students who lay among the lines of often mutilated bodies. He recalled in particular the fate of one particular Bolivian student who had entrusted him with a folder containing papers which he, the student, considered to be of great importance to his country. As a member of MIR (Movimiento de la Izquierda Revolucionaria) which was founded in 1971 by a merger of a left-wing faction of Bolivia's Christian Democratic Party and the radical student wing of MNR (Revolutionary Nationalist Movement), the student was well aware that he would be a person of interest to the military and was afraid that the folder might fall into the wrong hands.

Not long after taking possession of the folder Luis was visited by an army officer who advised him that the student had died following a fall from a window of the interrogation room. Luis questioned whether he had fallen, been thrown from the window or had jumped to his death rather than reveal information which would have put his friends in danger. Whatever the truth of the incident it was Luis's sad task to go to the National Stadium, where the man's wife was detained, to inform her of her husband's death. Years later, while teaching in Bolivia, he had occasion to return the folder to the man's wife who had eventually been released and had returned home to Bolivia.

Chileans in Scotland

Fortunately, due to the coordinated efforts of people sympathetic to the plight of their fellow colleagues - students and workers whose names figured on proscribed lists - many activists were able to avoid capture and to flee the country. I had the opportunity to speak to one such fortunate survivor of the widespread persecution of activists by the Chilean military when he addressed pupils at a meeting in St. Ambrose High School in Coatbridge, which was organised by the school in liaison with Father Willie Slavin of Justice and Peace, Scotland. Oscar Mendoza was a seventeen-year old student of economics and sociology at the University when he joined Salvador Allende's Socialist Party and the centre-left coalition Popular Unity government. He was forced to flee Chile and to seek asylum in Scotland after the coup d'état. He will not remember me, but I clearly remember a conversation we had which has stayed with me all these years. This was at a time when economic policies introduced by the Thatcher Government were ravaging Scotland's industrial base. The Labour Party was in disarray and I could see no end to Tory rule, a dismal prospect. Oscar's response to my gloomy outlook was to remind me that "Nothing is forever". Here was a man who had escaped the most repressive regime in Chile's history and yet still remained positive about the future. That simple statement continued to sustain me even when Trump was trashing treaties designed to promote peace and protect the planet and was retreating into isolationism, threatening to build walls instead of bridges.

Most of the political activists, who were fortunate enough to escape the country crossed into Peru and Argentina when the brutal repression began, immediately following the coup. However, thousands more made their way to various countries in Europe. Following negotiations with the UN High Commission for Refugees, the UK agreed to accept 3000 Chilean refugees who were then dispersed throughout Britain. Of these, 500 found their way to a life in Scotland. Oscar Mendoza was but one of them. Another was Carlos Arredondo who became a popular singer-songwriter and political and cultural campaigner. In an interview on BBC Radio Scotland's *'Songs of Courage'* programme he explained that people in his barrio very quickly became aware that many of their neighbours were suddenly disappearing:

"When I was living in Glasgow, I learned about the killing of five of my friends who were members of the same organisation I used to belong to - a Catholic youth organisation."

Just as they had done during the Spanish Civil War, ordinary working people all over Scotland rallied to the support of the refugees. Scottish Aid for Spain and the Spanish Medical Programme had their counterparts in the Chile Defence Committee and the Chile Solidarity Campaign which brought together the efforts of local people in towns and cities around Scotland. An article in The Herald, 11 June 2013, written by Brian Donnelly highlighted the part played by Scottish miners in sponsoring the escape of Chilean activists and referred specifically to the case of Sonia Leal, a social worker living in Edinburgh who, as a seven year old, was among the refugees who arrived in

Cowdenbeath in 1973. Her account of the reception the exiles received the day of their arrival in the Fife town described a scene which contrasts sharply with the way immigrants are received in some parts of Britain today:

"It was amazing. The miners' band played when we arrived, and everything was there for us. They had put loads of blankets in the houses as they thought we would be cold. The whole town put in for Christmas presents and I got a guitar."

Not that everything was rosy for all the refugees. Roger Kennedy, a close friend and colleague, also a Spanish graduate, who taught in a South Lanarkshire High School at the time, recounted to me the contrasting experiences of dealings he had with two refugee families. One of the men had been a miner and being as tough as nails gave the impression that he was able to survive whatever life threw at him. He quickly adapted to his new surroundings and Roger's only real involvement with him was to accompany him on a visit to an excellent local doctor to ascertain the medical history of his children. The father of the other family was an extremely sensitive and highly educated man, an intellectual who found it very difficult to come to terms with the trauma of his exile and the situation in which he now found himself. "I saw his passport. It was stamped *'salida única',*" recalled Roger. He was allowed to leave Chile but was not allowed to return. A broken man, he was unable to cope with the situation in which he now found himself. He had been a civil engineer, responsible, among other things, for the construction of roads, bridges and dams. Once he had settled into his new home and enrolled his three children into the local High School, Roger took him to the local Social Security office where he completed the paper-work necessary for the receipt of benefits - a humiliating experience for him. That done, Roger took him to a local hotel where they chatted over a pint of beer. Little did Roger suspect what was to follow. When the man returned to his home, he consumed every pill in his house and ended up in hospital where he had to have his stomach pumped. Such was the state of his depression that he had to have psychiatric counselling.

Apart from the practical material support afforded the refugees in Scotland one group of workers opted for direct action against the Pinochet regime. Felipe Bustos Sierra, a Chilean film-maker, in his documentary *"Nae Pasarán"* tells the story of how, six months after the military coup d'état, four workers in the Rolls Royce factory in East Kilbride - Bob Fulton, Robert Somerville, John Keenan and Stuart Barrie - refused to service and repair engines for Hawker Hunter planes of the Chilean air-force similar to those used in the bombing of La Moneda, the presidential palace in Santiago. The boycott continued for four years with the engines lying in crates outside the factory, exposed to the elements, until they mysteriously disappeared, stolen in the middle of the night and spirited away in vehicles with false licence plates. *"It was as if the SAS had done it,"* opined Bob Fulton.

Of course, the workers could have been sacked for their protest and certainly today such an action would entail considerably more risk, so what prompted the boycott? The workers had already discussed the situation in Chile and had roundly condemned the Chilean junta. As John Keenan so succinctly put it:

"The people being tortured and murdered, many of them were just like us: trade unionists."

The common humanity of these working class men

contrasted sharply with the attitude of the Chilean military who despised and feared organised labour to such an extent that they were prepared to embark on a campaign of terror in order to browbeat into submission, not only trade unionists but also any political activists, artists or intellectuals who might be considered "dangerous." As a result of the research carried out by Felipe Bustos Sierra and his team in making the documentary, for their efforts in the field of human rights three of the workers - Bob Fulton, Robert Somerville and John Keenan - were given the Chilean Government's highest honour to be bestowed on foreigners. In 2015 they were conferred with the title of Commanders of the Republic of Chile –the Order of Bernardo O'Higgins.

What a pity the Scottish Football Authorities, and indeed so many Scottish International footballers, did not follow the example of these principled trade unionists. When the opportunity arose to demonstrate Scottish football's opposition to, and repudiation of, the murderous treatment of the regime's opponents, by refusing to play an international friendly match with Chile in the very stadium where so many were tortured and murdered, the SFA sanctioned the game, justifying their decision by declaring that politics should be kept out of football. (Appendix B)

Chapter 9

Joan Garcés and The Attempt to Extradite Pinochet

"Someone has to tell what happened here and only you can do it"
Salvador Allende to Joan Garcés

When Luis undertook to play a major part in the successful plan to get Joan Garcés safely out of Chile and away from the clutches of the army in September 1973 little did he know that, a quarter of a century later, his former colleague would play a prominent part in the attempt to extradite the Chilean dictator from London to Spain – Pinochet was arrested in the English capital in October 1998. This was not Pinochet's first visit to Britain which he regarded as his favourite country. During the 1990s he often visited the country as a guest of the arms industry and frequently met Margaret Thatcher who was a great admirer of the former Chilean dictator whom she considered to be a great friend of Britain having covertly assisted the country during the Falklands war.

However, when he arrived in London for an informal visit in September 1998 circumstances had changed. The Conservative Government had been replaced in 1997 by Tony Blair's Labour administration and, after ruling Chile with an iron fist for over 16 years, he had failed in his attempt to extend his rule for a further eight years by means of a national referendum held on 6th October 1988. Since he was now no longer a Head of State but rather a life Senator it was to become a matter of considerable legal debate as to whether he still enjoyed diplomatic immunity when travelling abroad.

The long running legal battle to have Pinochet extradited to Spain following his arrest in October 1998, which continued until 1 March 2000 when he was given the news that he could return to Chile, is described in great detail in Ernesto Ekaizer's excellent account of the ex-dictator's record in Chile following the military coup in 1973, and his arrest and subsequent release in London in March 2000. What follows here is my summary of the events leading up to Pinochet's release, but I cannot commend highly enough the detailed description of these events presented by Ernesto Ekaizer in his book "Yo, Augusto."

Joan Garcés, now president of the *Fundación Presidente Allende*, who had never ceased in his efforts to bring Pinochet to justice, saw the former dictator's visit to Britain as an opportunity to have him extradited to Spain to answer the charge of crimes against Spanish citizens in Chile. With a view to initiating proceedings against the former Chilean dictator, in 1986 Garcés had approached Carlos Castresana, a Madrid prosecutor who along with Carlos Slepoy, an Argentinian labour lawyer, President of the Argentinian Human Rights Association, had prepared similar charges against the Argentine military. The charges had been lodged with the Supreme Court in Madrid and the case was subsequently deemed to fall within Spanish jurisdiction by judge Baltasar Garzón who would later play a prominent part in the attempt to have Pinochet extradited to Spain. Garcés and Castresana began to gather the evidence necessary for the case against the senator.

Andy McEntee, the Scots lawyer President of the British section of Amnesty International, had been active in reporting human rights abuses in Chile since he began working for the Chilean Human Rights Committee in London in 1986. He was well aware of the fact that Pinochet had already visited Britain on several occasions and had been able to go about his business and leave without hindrance. It was his considered opinion that, if anything was to be done to get justice for the victims of the Chilean Military Junta, proceedings would have to be instigated by Spain.

He phoned Joan Garcés in Madrid and explained that, in the United Kingdom, only the police could issue an arrest warrant and that there was not enough evidence for them to do so. Since Judge Baltasar Garzón had been able to issue an arrest warrant for General Galtieri for crimes against Spanish citizens in Argentina, the best way to proceed would be to have a Spanish judge issue an international arrest warrant for Pinochet for crimes against Spanish citizens in Chile. Garcés agreed to consult with colleagues as to the best way to proceed. McEntee advised him that his (Garcés's) preferred option of including the crime of genocide was not one that could be pursued extraterritorially by the United Kingdom. However, Federico Andreu, lawyer for Amnesty International, did offer his support in any action which was taken in Spain.

What followed was a long drawn out legal battle over the possible extradition of Pinochet to Spain. After much debate and soul searching in Madrid, Judge Baltasar Garzón issued an international arrest warrant with a view to the extradition of Augusto Pinochet Ugarte which was sent to London via Interpol where the duty Metropolitan magistrate signed a warrant for his arrest, 16 October 1998. The arrest took place at The London Clinic where Pinochet had been admitted for an operation to his spinal column – the efforts in Chile to spirit the general out of the U.K. before his possible arrest were thus thwarted. Pinochet was furious claiming that he had diplomatic immunity as he was on a secret mission. "I know who is behind all this," he fulminated, "it is that communist Garcés."

Legal teams on both sides argued over the question of whether or not Pinochet enjoyed diplomatic immunity. However, the debate over the legal position with regard to immunity seemed to have become academic when the Supreme Court ruled that the order of arrest for the murder of Spanish citizens was illegal as it was not an extraditable offence in the U.K. Undeterred, Joan Garcés and his team feverishly worked to prepare further evidence and produce witnesses to the crimes committed by the Chilean Junta. These efforts resulted in a second order of arrest which included the crimes of torture and forced disappearance of individuals. This arrest warrant was also ruled out when, despite previous Home Office advice, it was ruled that Pinochet, as an ex-head of State, did in fact enjoy immunity from due legal process. An appeal against this ruling was then presented to the Appeals Committee of the House of Lords, 2 November. After considering the evidence from both sides it was agreed that the Law Lords would deliver their verdict on 25 November. Against all the expectations of Pinochet's entourage the Law Lords upheld the appeal and plans to immediately fly the dictator back to Chile had to be cancelled. However, the matter was far from definitively decided. It came to the attention of the senator's legal team that one of the Law Lords had links with Amnesty International, the British President of which had been assisting Joan Garcés prepare the case for extradition. The impartiality of the Law Lord was called into question and a further appeal to the Appeals Committee in the House of Lords was lodged which resulted in a decision to revisit the case by a different panel of Law Lords. The seven-man appeals committee ruled that Pinochet could be extradited but only on the charges of torture and conspiracy to torture committed after 8th December 1988. The final decision as to whether senator Pinochet should be extradited was now in the hands of the Home Secretary, Jack Straw. One of the many factors which the Home Secretary had to take into consideration was the apparent deterioration in the health of Pinochet since his operation – a factor which was to become decisive.

On 11th January 2000 Straw issued a statement on the report of a medical examination which Pinochet had undergone in order to determine the state of his health. According to the unanimous decision of the four-man team of medical experts who had conducted the examination the deterioration in Pinochet's health was such that he was in no condition to stand trial for extradition and that there was little prospect of any improvement in his physical condition. Given these findings, Straw concluded that there was no point in continuing extradition procedures. The reaction to this decision was predictable.

As was to be expected, Pinochet's entourage was elated - as was Margaret Thatcher who was one of the first to congratulate the Home Secretary on his decision. When the conclusions of the medical team - but not the reasons for them - were communicated to interested parties, those countries which had sought extradition - which apart from Spain, included France,

Belgium and Switzerland - argued that a complete version of the report should be made available to them. A successful appeal to the Supreme Court to have the full report made available to all interested parties led to a team of medical experts being assembled by Judge Garzón to study its findings. This commission's conclusions disagreed with the report's findings that Pinochet was unfit to stand trial. Despite all efforts, however, on 1 March 2000 Pinochet was given the news that he was free to leave the country. Prior to take off Pinochet was handed a gift from Margaret Thatcher – a reproduction of a plate made in 1588 to commemorate the victory of Sir Francis Drake over the Spanish Armada. The plate, a thinly veiled criticism of Spain, was signed *Margaret Thatcher.*

At the time I could hardly believe that Pinochet had once again escaped justice and was bitterly disappointed that it was a Labour Home Secretary who had ruled that he was free to return to Chile. Nor could I understand Margaret Thatcher's total admiration for such a murderous dictator. I have since come to understand that those with a messianic vision of how the world should be ruled see opponents as obstacles to the fulfilment of a mission and therefore expendable. In this regard Thatcher and Pinochet were kindred spirits.

Margaret Thatcher with her good friend Augusto Pinochet

Thatcher, Pinochet and the Chicago Boys

(Economics are the method; the object is to change the heart and soul.)
Margaret Thatcher

Given Luis's account of events in Chile and the evidence of countless witnesses of the horrors visited on the political opponents of the military junta, I remember asking myself at the time how Margaret Thatcher could possibly justify her admiration and gushing support for such a cold, calculated and ruthless dictator. The stated justification for her obsequious stance was Pinochet's support for Britain during the Falklands War in 1982 between the United Kingdom and Argentina over the two British dependent territories in the South Atlantic – the Falkland Islands and its dependency the South Georgia and South Sandwich Islands. It should be remembered, of course, that even before the outbreak of the Falklands war – in July 1980 to be precise – the Conservative government had reversed the decision by the previous Labour government to ban the sale of arms to Pinochet's regime. In truth, the General was returning the favour.

While Thatcher could readily describe Nelson Mandela, recipient of the Nobel Peace Prize in 1993, as a terrorist, she was fulsome in her praise of Pinochet, the man responsible for the death, systematic torture and disappearance of so many political opponents – real, suspected or imagined - referring to him as a great friend of Britain, and the man responsible for *" a new era in Chile founded on true democracy."* Orwellian language and fake news were around long before George W Bush and Tony Blair made their mendacious claim about weapons of mass destruction in order to justify the invasion of Iraq, or Donald Trump began his personal attacks on any reporter who dared challenge the veracity of his frequent, outrageous and puerile statements and tweets. The real purveyors of 'fake news' still strut the political stage.

However, what Thatcher most admired about Pinochet was not just the *fact* that the junta had overthrown Allende's socialist government but the *reason* why the military coup was felt necessary, not just by a Chilean élite but by corporate America with the support of the high echelons of the U.S government. *"The economy, stupid"* a phrase coined by Bill Clinton's campaign strategist, aptly and succinctly echoed Richard Nixon's order to 'make the (Chilean) economy scream.' The Allende government's introduction of socialist policies designed to improve the lot of ordinary Chileans did not go down well with corporate America. The multi-nationals were already unhappy with the nationalist economic policies which had been introduced by other Latin American countries in the Southern Cone which had secured a better standard of living for workers who were beginning to enjoy the benefits previously the prerogative of the middle classes. Such policies ate into profits to the annoyance of big business. In order to challenge these policies Chile became, under Pinochet, the first country in the world to adopt the fundamentalist laissez-faire economic policies taught to students at the University of Chicago's Economics Department under the chairmanship of Theodore W Schultz.

The background to the Department's opposition to existing Keynesian economics and to the increasingly left wing economic policies being introduced in Argentina, Uruguay, Chile and Brazil, and to the rise of the 'Chicago Boys' whose task would be to roll back these 'socialist' policies, is considered in great detail in Naomi Klein's excellent book " *The Shock Doctrine*". In response to the worldwide havoc caused by the Great Depression which began in the United States in the 1930's President Franklin D. Roosevelt's "New Deal" had introduced a series of public work projects, financial reforms and regulations the purpose of which was to alleviate the plight of the unemployed and the poor. The objective was to reform the financial system and to bring about economic recovery.   Such measures were anathema to the economic professors at the Chicago University's Economics Department. A particular critic of the New Deal was Milton Friedman one of the Department's most famous professors who argued that Roosevelt had set the world on the wrong economic path. He set out his stall in *"Capitalism and Freedom"*, which became the bible of neo-conservatives:

"First, governments must remove all rules and regulations standing in the way of the accumulation of

profits. Second, they should sell off any assets they own that corporations could be running at a profit. And third, they should dramatically cut back funding of social programs. Within the three-part formula of deregulation, privatization and cutbacks, Friedman had plenty of specifics. Taxes, when they must exist, should be low, and rich and poor should be taxed at the same flat rate. Corporations should be free to sell their products anywhere in the world, and governments should make no effort to protect local industries and local ownership. All prices, including the price of labour, should be determined by the market. There should be no minimum wage. For privatization, Friedman offered up health care, the post office, education, retirement pensions, even national parks. [20]*

This was the man who served as an adviser to the Thatcher government from 1979 to 1990, the period during which it developed a free-market economy, low taxation, and the sale of state-owned industries and he was the man to whom Pinochet turned for economic advice once all opposition had been defeated, intimidated or eliminated. Chile was to be the testing ground for the neo-liberal economic counter revolution. To assist in the implementation of the new policies, Pinochet brought on board many of the Chicago University's Economics Department trained Chilean students – the Chicago Boys - who had been sponsored by the U.S. government with a view to countering the economic policies of the countries in the Southern Cone.

The problem with the so-called "free market" is that it is only "free" for the rich. Buyers with unlimited

---

[20] Naomi Klein: The Shock Doctrine, p57

funds will always outbid poorer competitors and wealthy traders with their economic power have the advantage of being able to afford marketing strategies beyond the financial means of poorer rivals in the market. Take, for example, the case of the football transfer market. In the Scottish Premiership, teams in the lower half of the league cannot compete in the transfer market with the Big Two, Celtic and Rangers, and the Old Firm, in turn, cannot compete with the top English and European teams. In the wider market, large national and multi-national firms simply swallow up smaller firms and are able to move their operations to countries where the wages are low and where they can avoid taxes and legislation which they see as affecting profits. The market is a place of unfair competition where the wealthy seek maximum economic benefit at the expense of the less well off. The so-called 'free market' only exists in the speeches of neo-liberal economists and their political followers. As José Luis Sampedro explains:

"Given the enormous power of firms and economic groupings in the market it should be remembered that private interest does not always coincide with public interest. Firms pursue a prosperity based on the maximum possible gains while the common interest seeks a greater variety of aims often at the cost of sacrificing economic benefit – public health, education, respect for nature, aesthetic activities, social cohesion, compliance with ethical norms of co-existence among other manifestations of human existence. These are not the aims which are foremost in the businessman's mind." [21]

---

[21] José Luis Sampedro: El Mercado y la Globalización, p49

Chapter 10

Us and Them

If even on the basis of the crassest self-interest, we can realize that We and Them must be transcended in the totality of the human race, if We in destroying Them are not to destroy us all.

R.D.Laing

During talks I had with Luis about his experience in Sarajevo, capital of Bosnia-Herzogovina, which he visited as Head of a UNESCO delegation in December 1994, our conversation turned inevitably to a discussion of what R.D. Laing describes as an Us and Them mentality which has had such a devastating global effect on human relationships down through the ages. Historical examples of man's inhumanity to man resulting from divisions based on race, ethnicity, religion or class, have forever cast a deadly shadow over mankind.

As I have already referred to in the introduction to this study, there are historical examples aplenty of the horrendous effects of divisions between peoples and of intolerance of the *'Other.'* One need only consider the horrors inflicted on both Christians and Muslims during the Crusades, the Religious Wars in Europe, the Khmer Rouge killing fields in Kampuchea where more than a million people were killed and buried, the mass murder of more than six million Jews by the German Nazi regime during the period 1941-1945, the Rwandan Genocide in which 500,000 to 1,000,000 Tutsi were slaughtered by members of the Hutu majority in 1994, the ongoing conflicts in the Middle East between Israelis and Palestinians and between Sunni and Shia Muslims, and, nearer home, the Troubles in Northern Ireland between Unionists and Nationalists. The list is endless and yet we never seem to learn.

The United Nations Educational, Scientific and Cultural Organization (UNESCO) to which Luis has dedicated so many years of his life, was established in November 1946 with the specific aim of combatting through education this Us and Them mentality. The aim of the organization was to create the conditions necessary for dialogue between civilizations, cultures and peoples based on mutual respect. The Preamble to the UNESCO Constitution addressed the root causes of the destructive differences between peoples in the belief that only through education could they be overcome.

Preamble

The Governments of the States Parties to this Constitution on behalf of their peoples declare:

That since wars begin in the minds of men, it is in the minds of men that the defences of peace must be constructed;

That ignorance of each other's ways and lives has been a common cause, throughout the history of mankind, of that suspicion and mistrust between the peoples of the world through which their differences have all too often broken into war;

That the great and terrible war which has now ended was a war made possible by the denial of the democratic principles of the dignity, equality and mutual respect of men, and by the propagation, in their place, through ignorance and prejudice, of the doctrine of the inequality of men and races;

That the wide diffusion of culture, and the education of humanity for justice and liberty and peace are indispensable to the dignity of man and constitute a sacred duty which all the nations must fulfil in a spirit of mutual assistance and concern;

That a peace based exclusively upon the political and economic arrangements of governments would not be a peace which could secure the unanimous, lasting and sincere support of the peoples of the world, and that the peace must therefore be founded, if it is not to fail, upon the intellectual and moral solidarity of mankind;

For these reasons, the States Parties to this Constitution, believing in full and equal opportunities for education for all, in the unrestricted pursuit of objective truth, and in the free exchange of ideas and knowledge, are agreed and determined to develop and to increase the means of communication between their peoples and to employ these means for the purpose of mutual understanding and a truer and more perfect knowledge of each other's lives;

In consequence whereof they do hereby create the United Nations Educational, Scientific and Cultural Organization for the purpose of advancing, through the educational and scientific and cultural relations of the peoples of the world, the objectives of international peace and of the common welfare of mankind for which the United Nations Organization was established and which its Charter proclaims.

Who could disagree with the sentiments expressed in this Preamble and yet over seventy years on from the foundation of UNESCO the organization still faces an uphill struggle to have them universally accepted. The daunting task facing UNESCO, indeed any educationist intent on developing independent thinking, is graphically highlighted by Jason Burke's account of the situation in those schools recently under Islamic State control where,

"education is seen as part of a campaign not just to win 'hearts and minds' but to 'reform' them. Some government schools continue to function, with their original staff, but with strict segregation of teachers and students and a curriculum purged of more or less anything but study of the Koran, the deeds and sayings of the Prophet and Islamic law. Foreign languages, mathematics, social sciences and references to nation states have all been banned from lessons. The long-term aim is the quintessence of totalitarianism: to eliminate all possibility of alternative viewpoints, particularly among the young, and to raise a new generation of utterly loyal, unquestioning 'citizens' of the caliphate."[22]

However, as was discovered in Cuba, where Che Guevara's well-intentioned idea of creating '*el hombre nuevo*', for whom the incentive to work and the purpose of life would not be the egotistical accumulation of material wealth but rather the moral and altruistic obligation to society in general, theoretical ideas are far from easy to put into practice. The difficulty for those who seek to create homogeneous societies is that, like it or not:

"any vision dedicated to eradicating difference and diversity is always going to find the reality of human

---

[22] Jason Burke: The New Threat from Islamic Militancy, p98

society something of a challenge."[23]

Not that the alternative, co-existence, does not present its own challenges.

As UNESCO's long experience in the field of education has shown, the difficulty with efforts to foster a better understanding of cultural differences is that they are not always universally well received especially when they are regarded as concessions to 'Them.' In 1984, for example, the Reagan administration in the U.S. withdrew from UNESCO citing a bias towards the Soviet Union, while in January 2019, the U.S. and Israel pulled out of the organization alleging anti-Israel bias due to UNESCO having declared Hebron, the historical city in the Israeli-occupied West Bank, an endangered world heritage site.

The Breakup of Yugoslavia

"I watched close at hand as the leaders of various peoples, be they Serbian, Croat or Bosniak, deliberately reminded their 'tribes' of the ancient divisions and, yes, ancient suspicions in a region crowded with diversity. Once they had pulled the peoples apart, it didn't take much to then push them against each other."[24]

Nowhere does the horror of conflicts resulting from the clash of cultures manifest itself with such appalling consequences as in countries which formerly made up the Socialist Federation of Yugoslavia (1945-1991). The Yugoslav Constitution established six constituent Socialist Republics in the Federation: Bosnia-

---

[23] Ibid, p93
[24] Tim Marshall: Prisoners of Geography, Introduction, p, ix

Herzegovina, Croatia, Macedonia, Montenegro, Serbia and Slovenia - Serbia also had two autonomous provinces: Kosovo and Vojvodina. The chief architect of the Federation was Josip Broz Tito (1892-1980) who had been the partisan leader during the struggle against the Germans and Italians who had occupied and partitioned Yugoslavia in 1941. His attempt, in the 1974 constitution, to introduce greater equality among the six republics and Serbia's autonomous regions did not go down well with Serbia and Croatia, the republics with the largest populations. Serbia was particularly unhappy with the independent role given to its two autonomous regions and the recognition and indeed promotion of minority identity especially of the Albanians in Kosovo.

It was never going to be an easy task to hold together such a disparate group of republics and the resentment which had been bubbling over in Tito's later years quickly came to a head in the years after his death. The inevitable disintegration of the Socialist Federation of Yugoslavia began In June 1991 when Slovenia and Croatia declared independence, followed in January 1992 by Macedonia and in April of the same year by Bosnia-Herzegovina. Serbia and Montenegro also broke away in 1992, forming the Federal Republic of Yugoslavia which was later reconstituted as the State Union of Serbia and Montenegro before an independence referendum in Montenegro resulted in the two republics becoming separate countries.

However, the vote for independence in Bosnia-Herzegovina in 1992, far from stabilising the region, merely led inevitably to the outbreak of civil war. Bosnia-Herzegovina had three major and competing ethnic groups: Bosniaks, who were ethnically Muslim and constituted the largest group, Bosnian Serbs, who were mainly Orthodox Christians and Bosnian Croats who were primarily Catholic – a classic Us and Them tinderbox. Bosniaks and Bosnian Croats were in favour of independence, but Bosnian Serbs boycotted the referendum or were prevented from taking part by Bosnian Serb authorities. Encouraged by Serbian re-centralists, Bosnian Serbs argued that Bosnia-Herzegovina should join with Serbia, an idea which was anathema to Bosniaks and Bosnian Croats. The Bosnian Serbs, led by Radovan Karadzic and supported by the Serbian government of Slobodan Milosevic and the Yugoslav People's Army, mobilised inside Bosnia-Herzegovina to protect ethnic Serb territory.

The Bosnian war which followed, and the Croat/Bosniak war, which came to be referred to as the war within a war, were brutal and bloody inter-ethnic conflicts, one of the worst examples of which was the deliberate policy of ethnic cleansing and genocide against Bosniaks perpetrated by the Bosnian Serb military and the Scorpions, a Serbian paramilitary force. This was the conflict which resulted in the execution in Srebrenica, in north eastern Bosnia, of more than 8,000 Bosniak men and boys. The massacre took place despite the fact that the area had been designated a safe area by the U.N. and nominally under the protection of a contingent of Dutch soldiers.

Apart from the horrors of the Srebrenica genocide, there was the brutalising effect of daily intimidation, denial of human rights, forced expatriation of ethnic opponents and attacks on major cities, all of which resulted in approximately 100,000 deaths and 1,000,000 refugees. The siege of Sarajevo, capital of Bosnia-Herzegovina, from 5th April 1992 to 29 February 1996, by the Yugoslav Peoples' army and later by the Army of Republika Srbija, was the longest in the history of modern warfare and the subject of several conversations I had with Luis.

Chapter 11

Luis in Sarajevo and Kosovo

As war continues, both sides come more and more to resemble each other. The uroboros eats its own tail. The wheel turns full circle. Shall we realize that We and Them are shadows of each other? We are Them to Them as They are Them to Us.

R.D.Laing

The war in Bosnia-Herzegovina, apart from resulting in thousands of deaths and a million displacements, also resulted in many psychotic and social breakdowns among the military participants and, in particular, the civilian population. The stress and mental health problems resulting from the war were considered in a project "Psycho-social aspects of war in Bosnia-Herzegovina" which was carried out by the Academy of Sciences and Arts of Bosnia-Herzegovina and the Department of Psychiatry of the Clinical Centre of Sarajevo University. Findings of the study indicated that there was a strong link between the very low socio-economic level of the inhabitants of Sarajevo and the potential of absolute poverty, due mainly to low level of education, very poor living standards, bad health and unemployment. Of particular concern for UNESCO, as the U.N. organisation responsible for education, was the marked increase in neurotic and psychotic disorders among children and adolescents. For Federico Mayor Zaragoza, Spanish scientist, politician and poet, who served as Director General of UNESCO between 1987 and 1999, recognition by all concerned of the fact that the sine qua non of peaceful co-existence and the avoidance of internecine struggles is that:

"the implementation of a culture of peace project requires a thorough mobilization of all means of education, both formal and non-formal and of communication"[25]

Just how to implement such a culture in war-torn Bosnia-Herzogovina was the major headache facing the Director General. In particular, there was mounting pressure to find a solution to the problem of schooling, or lack of it, and the protection of cultural activities, in a country ravaged by war.

Luis Ramallo, as Head of a UNESCO delegation, arrived in Sarajevo on New Year's Eve 1994. The town had been under siege since 5 April 1992 and at the time of the delegation's arrival it was still under constant bombardment by Serb forces located in the hills surrounding the city. Luis was charged by the Director General with the task of weighing up the situation and reporting back to UNESCO Headquarters in Paris. He arrived at the airport in a Russian transport plane with UN soldiers – Swedish troops with French officers - who were there to act as observers only. They disembarked directly into a protective tunnel leading to the terminal, a necessary precaution due to the fighting which was raging all around the airport. There Luis received a report of the military situation by the UN observer on the ground before heading to his hotel in an armoured car and wearing the compulsory flak-jacket and UN protective helmet.

His remit was to ascertain the effect the war was

---

[25] As stated in the Formal Conclusions from the First International Forum on the Culture of Peace

having on the cultural life and education in the city. His first port of call was the site of the National and University Library located in what had been originally the Sarajevo City Hall, Vijecnica, before it was handed over to the National Library. On 25 August 1992 the Library had been destroyed during the shelling of Sarajevo by Serb forces. As a result of the bombardment of the building, and despite the efforts of librarians and members of the public, hundreds of manuscripts were lost, as were most of the library's books, many of which were extremely rare, irreplaceable old copies.

He next visited the Academy of Sciences and Arts of Bosnia-Herzegovina, the city's principle centre of intellectual activity which was responsible for the development of science and the arts, organizing cultural events and publishing academic papers written by members. There the staff stressed to Luis that, although, of course, they appreciated the need for material aid, one of their main concerns was the lack of news and reading material, a fact which Luis was to include in his report along with his recommendation that newspapers and reading material should be an important part of the aid being sent to the beleaguered city.

His fact-finding tour next took him to the Children's Hospital where he was able to see for himself, not only the horrific physical injuries inflicted on the children of Sarajevo by Serbian shelling and sniper fire, but also the psychological affect the conflict was having on their mental health and, of course, their education. He knew that, if any progress was to be made in healing the ethnic divisions which were the root cause of the war in Bosnia, the education of the younger generation would be of paramount importance. It was disheartening to witness the carnage which resulted from the shelling of innocent children and to know that their suffering at the hands of another ethnic group would almost certainly reinforce and perpetuate the divisions in many young minds which had been passed down from generation to generation. To overcome such historical divisions would require long term educational planning and commitment.

A Meeting in the Mountains

It did not take Luis long to realise just how dangerous was the situation in which he now found himself. In his hotel on one occasion he found it necessary to place items of furniture behind the door of his room for fear of attack by a group of Serb fighters on the floor below, a fear which kept him awake and on edge all night. UN positions were not immune from the shelling and Serbian soldiers in the hills were denying aid agencies permission to enter Sarajevo with relief supplies. Even UN convoys were being denied clearance to move in and out of the city. Such was the blatant disregard for the UN that Luis was compelled to give an order to the affect that the UN flag should not be flown on buildings for fear that they were being targeted.

The situation in the besieged city was so bad that Luis, despite the possible danger to his own safety, sought a meeting with the Serbian commander in the mountains. His Slovenian interpreter was most uneasy and reluctant to accompany him to any such meeting and so Luis instructed him to go instead and speak to reporters of the local daily newspaper in the hope that he might be able to gather some useful information about the situation on the ground from their local knowledge. *"Oslobodenje"*, the only paper still operating in Sarajevo was by then working out of a bomb shelter after its ten-storey office building had been destroyed with the loss of five lives and many injuries to staff members.

During the hour-long journey into the mountains in an armoured car Luis became more and more apprehensive, wondering what he had gotten himself into and questioning the wisdom of his decision to arrange such a meeting and in such a remote place. When he finally arrived at the Serb positions, he was informed that the commander was unavailable to meet him but that his education spokesman would be happy to discuss his concerns. The so-called cultural expert, while obviously keen to give the impression of being *au fait* with all matters relating to education, was in full combat dress and armed to the teeth, a fact which did nothing to alleviate the anxiety felt by Luis or give him confidence that much could be achieved during their discussions. Indeed, during the hour-long meeting he was subjected to a long diatribe about Serb grievances and an explanation of what he described as the Serb side of the story. When he eventually left the Serb positions, while relieved to be heading back safely to Sarajevo, Luis was of the opinion that little, if anything, had been achieved by the visit.

Kosovo

When the 1974 Yugoslav constitution recognised the autonomous status of Kosovo, giving the province *de facto* self-government, it created a simmering resentment among Serbians which, after the break-up of Yugoslavia, led eventually to the Serbian President, Slobodan Milosevic stripping Kosovo of its autonomy in 1989 - a decision which led ethnic Albanian leaders in Kosovo to declare the country's independence from

Serbia in 1990. Milosevic's response was to launch a brutal crackdown on Kosovo's Albanian population which was only brought to an end by NATO military intervention in 1999. During interviews with the authors Marie-Francoise Allain and Xavier Galmiche, recorded in his book 'La question du Kosovo', the first President of Kosovo, Ibrahim Rugova - sometimes dubbed the "Gandhi of the Balkans" due to his advocacy of non-violent opposition to political injustices - described the system installed in Kosovo after the suspension of the country's autonomy as one of the most coercive in Europe. In a withering criticism of a system in which the over 90% Albanian majority was completely dominated by the minority Serb population and the authorities in Belgrade, Rugova declared:

"We are without work, without medical care, without banks, without radio or television and without the slightest power in law. Even the local Albanian police force, which only had 3,000 men, has been disbanded and the Pristina prison guards are all Serbs.....Education in the schools and the university is forbidden. Theatres and cinemas have been closed. Social and cultural life has been destroyed..... Albanians are excluded from all areas of life. At all levels. You can say that there is a total discrimination against them. We are suffering the effects of a massive daily terror....In three years 300,000 Albanians have emigrated to countries in western Europe. What we have here is silent "ethnic cleansing"[26]

UNESCO had received many complaints about the behaviour of the Serb authorities towards the Albanian population in Kosovo and about the brutality of the Serb army and paramilitaries. Luis made three separate

---

[26] Ibrahim Rugova: La Question du Kosovo, pp 54/55

visits to Kosovo in his capacity as Head of the UNESCO Delegation with the express remit of witnessing for himself the effects of Serbian political and military dominance on the social, educational and cultural life of the country. His visits to the capital, Pristina - which entailed a hazardous journey through Serbian territory - were revealing. What he discovered during his visits to almost 20 schools was that, in a country were the population was overwhelmingly Albanian, pupils of that ethnicity were not allowed to use their own language. In the schools he visited he found a two-tier system of education in which Serbian students were taught in the morning and the Bosnian Albanians attended classes in the afternoon.

After the abolition of Kosovo's autonomy, a new curriculum had been introduced into the education system which concentrated on Serbian culture and history and which made Serbo-Croatian a compulsory subject in Kosovo High Schools. Anyone wishing to enter a secondary school had to pass a Serbian Language test. Indeed, after 1992 in secondary schools and the University of Pristina, Serbian was the only language of instruction which meant that the Albanian language was only used in elementary schools. Before the creation of the parallel school system 20,000 secondary age pupils were among the thousands of Albanians forced to emigrate. In order to circumvent this discriminatory education policy Kosovo Albanians established a parallel system of education which allowed approximately 300-350,000 students to boycott state schools to attend the parallel Albanian-language private schools which were often located in mosques or private houses. Of course, pupils opting to attend these private schools were barred from entering the University of Pristina.

Chapter 12

Us and Them – The Orange and the Green

"For the strangers came and tried to teach us their
way,
They scorned us just for being what we are,
But they might as well go chasing after moonbeams,
Or light a penny candle from a star"

A. Cohalan

No Scottish writer, especially one from an Irish Catholic background, who wants to be taken seriously, can limit discussion of divisions among peoples to those in other countries when religious differences continue to be problematic in Scotland where the authorities have on more than one occasion had to ban political marches due to the serious possibility of violent street clashes between rival factions. It has to be said, of course, that the scale of the problem in Scotland in no way compares in intensity with the conflicts which we have already discussed, but one only need consider the recent Troubles in Northern Ireland between Unionists and Nationalists and the tenuous peace agreement there, to understand that there is no room for complacency, especially when, as I have already pointed out, there are always groups or individuals only too ready to exploit divisions.

The situation in Scotland has improved greatly over the years but given the cancer of sectarianism which still exists in certain areas and which manifests itself most openly at football matches, any writer prepared to discuss the problem must expect his/her partiality to be called into question in certain quarters. As the Glasgow historian Charles A Oakley so rightly pointed out:

"There is no subject which writers and speakers about Glasgow are less willing to tackle than that of the Irish in Scotland." [27]

Aware of the very possible charge of partiality, it would be easy to set aside the historical divisions in Ireland and Scotland, knowing full well that no matter how hard one endeavours to set aside any possible biased tendencies there will always be the accusation of failure to be impartial. However, since the whole idea behind the decision to write this book was to record the conversations of two octogenarians about their experiences of conflicts resulting from class, race, cultural or religious differences and the devastation such conflicts have caused to the lives of ordinary people, it could hardly be expected that the author should fail to discuss the divisions - and the root causes of these divisions – which have affected the lives of his ancestors in Ireland and which he has experienced, to a much lesser extent, in his own country.

The historical reasons for the fraught relationships between rival communities in Ireland will be considered in the next chapter but for now I believe it is important that the reader know something of my own family history in as much as it relates to one side of the political and religious divide in Ireland. I make no apologies for my Irish Catholic ancestry but, coming from a working class background, I am well aware that in the circles I moved in during my formative years, prejudices - often arrived at on the basis of hearsay and

---

[27] John Burrowes: Irish, The Remarkable Saga of a nation and a City. Preface, p9

the deliberate dissemination of untruths - were passed down from generation to generation to the exclusion of any possibility of impartiality.

Curious to know more about my own family history, I once took the opportunity to sit down with my mother to record as many details as she could remember about her own background. Her mother was born in Killygullib Glebe and her father in Laragh, townlands in the district of Kilrea, County Derry, one of the six Ulster Counties which now constitute Northern Ireland. I remember quite vividly, even now at the age of eighty, the many happy holidays I had at my mother's relatives' farm where cousin Jane tended to old uncle Joe, her bedridden father, and still found time to make us feel at home. To me, as a young boy, cousins Robert-John and Patrick seemed huge, powerful men whom you would not want to get on the wrong side of if they became angry. Not that they ever did as far as I can remember. Indeed, Patrick would often take me on the handlebars of his bicycle to the fields where we would cut peat to be stored in the barn for winter fuel. Those were happy days, when my sister Anne and I would go over to another cousin's farm to play with the children, one of whom, John Joseph, subsequently became a priest. Only rarely was there ever any mention of sectarian division even though the nearby farm was owned by a couple who were, I believe, members of the Orange Order. There was only the occasional warning from cousin Jane not to antagonise the police and in particular the "B Specials" - recently my brother-in-law John told me about conversations he had with my mother in which she revealed that she was often stopped in the street by "B Specials" when she was returning from a night out with friends.

As I was only nine when my father was killed in a mining accident, I never did have the opportunity to quiz him in the same way - not that he would have been as amenable to the same type of questioning. As far as I have been able to ascertain from records my great grandfather, Bernard Rooney, was a farmer born in Ireland although from where specifically I have no record – a late cousin was of the opinion that he might have been originally from Sligo. Despite the Irish background of my grandparents, however, there was never any discussion at home about the sectarian difficulties existing in both Ireland and Scotland. All I remember, as a boy, was that my mother would never allow me to wear the colours of Glasgow Celtic FC – the club founded by an Irish Marist, Brother Walfrid, born in Ballymote, County Sligo, in order to ameliorate the desperate conditions in which the working-class Irish immigrant community in the east end of Glasgow found itself in the 1880's. Although I wasn't fully aware of it as a young boy, the reason that I was not allowed to wear my team's colours was my mother's fear that I might come to some harm because of the anti-Irish racism of many people in the city. Keeping a low profile was her way of keeping us under the radar. It was a if we had to hide our ethnicity in order to be accepted by the majority population. Multiculturism was not a concept understood by some.

It wasn't until she was well into her eighties, and only when quizzed by me during the recorded conversations we had, that she opened up about some of the negative experiences she had when she visited Ireland with her brother, my uncle Pat:

"Pat and I used to go over to Ireland, and it would probably have been about 1922 when I first learned about the Black and Tans. We used to get off the boat

in Belfast about 6 a.m. and would go to the house of the McLeans, who were friends or relatives of my mother, until it was time to catch the train to Kilrea. There was an old man in the house with his two daughters and a young boy, Tom, who lives in Glasgow now I believe. On the way to the house we saw armoured cars everywhere. When we arrived, we could hear the iron bars and jam jars being moved from behind the door once they were certain it was us. The Tans were after the boy, so he had disappeared. The family had no idea where he was. The two girls and the old man later came over to Glasgow on the Ferry. The girls, who came to see us in Malcolm Street, were only lassies at the time but they're both dead now. I don't know about the boy who also came over to Glasgow eventually, but I never saw him again. I suppose he will be dead too."

It was only when I left school when I turned sixteen and began to look for employment that I gradually became aware that there was something of a problem. Securing employment proved to be no straightforward matter for a pupil with an identifiable catholic education unless of course that pupil was prepared to settle for a labouring job which I was forced to do for some considerable time. Even when in employment there were the constant pejorative references to my background and perceived lower social status. However, I soon realised that such attempts to belittle and embarrass me, progressively became fewer when met with the indifference of someone secure in the knowledge that the disparaging remarks revealed more about the insecurity and ignorance of the person making them than about myself. Not that the use of jibes and pejorative comments was restricted to what was often dismissed as harmless banter between workers. I remember once being out socially with a good friend, who happened to be Protestant, when a third party in our company, a civil engineer, remarked with just a hint of sarcasm that he had never met an articulate Catholic. He had obviously been used to overseeing Irish labourers. He might have benefitted from a little not-so-light reading on the subject of the contribution those same labourers made to the economic growth of Scotland:

"The fact that the Industrial Revolution did gather pace in Scotland, and that Glasgow and central Scotland were to become the workshop of the Empire, was in no small measure due to that huge reservoir of labour which arrived from Ireland. Without that special breed of readily mobile and accommodating worker, the new harbours, canals, railways, roads and hydro-electric schemes would not have been completed on the same scale. Without them, Scotland would be a smaller and less accomplished nation and Glasgow would never have become the city we know today."[28]

Prejudice and division have existed in Ireland and Scotland for generations and many people are confused as to why, in the form of sectarianism, they are still as toxic and dangerous as ever among certain sections of our communities. Personally, I refuse to play the Us and Them game. I have too many good friends of both persuasions. If we are ever to move forward constructively and peacefully it is important to consider the grievances, real or perceived, of *both* communities. The roots of the present-day problems lie deep in the past, of course, as we will discuss in the following chapter.

---

[28] John Burrowes: Irish: The Remarkable Saga of a Nation and a City, Preface pp12-13

Chapter 13

The Orange and the Green – Historic Ireland

"There never was, I believe, an Irish crime – if crime it can be called – which had not its roots in an English folly"
Redmond Howard

In order to better understand something of the historical grievances Irish people have against the English, why these grievances are buried so deep in the Irish psyche and why Protestant suspicions and fears of Irish Nationalism persist to this day, some understanding of Irish history is required. Stafford Reynolds of 'Building Communities'- a project set up to explore events surrounding the Great Famine - echoed my own strong feelings about the current sectarian divisions in Ireland when he stated that:

"We cannot aspire to a shared future, if we don't first develop a shared understanding of the past."

Of course, the task of persuading people with deeply ingrained prejudices, which in Ireland and Scotland have been passed down from generation to generation, is a particularly daunting one. However, it is important to appreciate, as did Jason Burke when writing about another, modern-day conflict, that:

"Trying to understand does not imply any sympathy. It simply means we set aside our very natural anger, disgust and fear in order, as dispassionately as possible, to learn. We need, above all, to avoid the trap that the extremists have fallen into, that of shutting

ourselves off, of closing our minds, of succumbing to the temptation of wilful ignorance."[29]

Historical Divisions

Most bloody conflicts between peoples have their origins in history. Over more than 800 years Ireland has suffered a series of incursions and disasters, the effects of which are still being felt today on the streets, not only of Ireland, but to a lesser extent of Scotland. Many eminent scholars have written minutely researched histories of Ireland and have considered, in detail, the problems which have arisen due to decisions taken by past English kings and governments and I recommend the works listed in the bibliography of this volume to any scholar interested in the subject.

However, for the purpose of the present study I have concentrated on particularly significant historical events in the turbulent history of the country in order to give some explanation as to why age-old divisions persist to this day. These events include the Anglo-Norman Invasion (1169-1171), The Reformation as it affected Ireland, the Irish Plantation, the Amended Penal Laws, the Great Famine (1845-1851), the struggle for Home Rule and the Easter Rising (1916). As I have already indicated, these events have been considered in great detail by eminent historians, and in much greater depth than the following summary of events. My purpose in considering them here is to try to offer some explanation as to why they have left such a lasting legacy of bitterness between some sectors of Catholic and Protestant communities in Ireland - and

---

[29] Jason Burke: The New Threat from Islamic Militancy. Introduction, pp12-13

to a lesser extent in Scotland - a legacy of *Us and Them* which makes any attempt at reconciliation and understanding all the more difficult.

The Anglo-Norman Invasion

When, in 1166, the provincial kings of Ireland rose against, deposed and dispossessed Dermot MacMurrough, King of Leinster and High King of Ireland, he sailed to England and sought the assistance of the Norman king, Henry II, in putting down his rivals, offering allegiance to the English crown in return. Pope Adrian IV, the English Pope who ruled the Papal States between 1154 until his death in 1159, had earlier sanctioned an invasion of Ireland by Henry, ostensibly to root out the vicious habits and loose morals of the native Irish. So not only were the Anglo Normans invited into the country, but the invasion had been legitimised by the Pope.

The first major force of Normans led by Richard Fitz Gilbert de Clare, Strongbow, arrived in County Wexford in 1170 and quickly put down opposition in Waterford. When Strongbow married Dermot's daughter and made himself King of Leinster on her father's death, Henry, fearing his subject was becoming too powerful and over ambitious, raised a strong force and sailed to confront Strongbow and the Norman barons and to establish his own authority over Ireland. The Anglo-Norman invasion saw the beginning of the great Irish land grab which continued through the late twelfth and thirteenth centuries when English kings used Irish land to reward loyal followers. While it is also true that the Normans introduced the parliamentary system of government to Ireland and a legal system based on English Common Law, as well as the English Language, the truth is Anglo Norman writ never extended to large parts of the country and so these innovations were never universally observed. Gaelic Ireland did not owe allegiance to the crown or English institutions and there was neither the appetite nor men enough in England to proceed to full colonisation. When the Plague was introduced to the Port of Howth in 1345 and many Norman lords fled back to England, there was a revival of Gaelic Irish culture and by the fifteenth century,

"the now famous English Pale reflected contemporary political and cultural realities in Ireland. This fortified line marked out and signified the area around Dublin within which English rule truly functioned. Beyond this boundary, as long as the nominal authority of the king was respected, practical power was of necessity left to rest with local powerful magnates. At the end of the fifteenth century this English Pale – the area within which English law, custom, language and culture flourished in Ireland – was a region which had shrunk to a comparatively small area around Dublin itself."[30]

The Reformation

Unlike the Protestant Reformation which spread through much of Europe following Martin Luther's feud with the Catholic Church, the English Reformation owed less to the attraction of theological reforms than to King Henry VIII's failure to obtain the annulment of his twenty-four year marriage to Catherine of Aragon in order to marry Anne Boleyn. Henry's break from the authority of Rome and the

---

[30] Richard English: Irish Freedom, p45

1536 Act of Supremacy which declared him supreme head of the Church in England, led to the adoption of Protestantism as the formal religion of the country and its gradual acceptance as such by the majority of the people. However, as was so succinctly put by Diarmaid MacCulloch, British historian and author of works on the Reformation and the History of Christianity:

"The contrast in religious outcome between England and the other Tudor kingdom of Ireland could hardly be greater: in Ireland, official Protestantism became the élite sect and Roman Catholicism the popular religion, in a result unique in the whole Reformation. In no other polity where a major monarchy made a long-term commitment to the establishment of Protestantism was there such a failure."[31]

The Tudor monarchs did not have the necessary will to vigorously press ahead with religious reforms and only intermittently turned their attention to the implementation of the Reformation in Ireland. Even if they had considered it a priority to do so they had neither the means nor the manpower to influence the majority Catholic population, especially in the more remote parts of the island, nor were they able to enlist the support of the local Gaelic and pre-Reformation English Catholic élites.

The Plantation of Ireland

Plantation was a Tudor scheme for reform in Ireland which was pursued with considerably more energy by the Stuart monarchs who succeeded Elizabeth I. Designed to make Ireland more British, to consolidate

---

[31] Richard English: Irish Freedom, p46

the new religion and, hopefully to civilise the indigenous population through the example of Protestant settlers - considered much more upright - it involved enticing English and Scottish Protestants to settle in Ireland with the promise of Irish land. Some of the early attempts at plantation, such as that in parts of County Down, were unsuccessful as they failed to attract settlers in sufficient numbers. Crown projects were more successful in numerical terms. By the middle of the seventeenth century 20,000 English Protestants had settled in Munster while 15,000 English and Scots had made their homes in Ulster. However, the influx of so many foreigners had predictable consequences, not least of which was the subsequent development of Irish nationalism. Given that the Irish depended on land for sustenance and the land was, just as during the Norman invasion, being allocated to strangers who not only regarded the Irish as uncivilised but who were also an integral part of the mission to eradicate Catholicism, how could it have been otherwise?

"Land in Counties Donegal, Armagh, Cavan, Fermanagh, Londonderry and Tyrone was divided into variously sized plots and granted to the incomers, who then lived in newly established Protestant clusters. The Ulster model involved the Plantation community as the explicit, distinct focus for the establishment of a British Ireland: they would be self-contained communities set apart from the dislocated Irish, the latter being excluded."[32]

The immediate consequence of the implementation of this colonising policy was a revolt by the indigenous catholic population against Plantation. The rebellion

---

[32] Richard English: Irish Freedom, p59

began in Ulster in 1641 and spread quickly throughout the island. In the sectarian massacres which followed, an estimated 4,000 settlers were killed. The horror of these events inevitably left an indelible mark on Ulster Protestants, just as the later military incursions of Cromwell's army would have on Irish Catholics.

A mere eight years after the events of 1641, Oliver Cromwell became Lord Protector of the Commonwealth and was selected to take command of the English campaign in Ireland as Lord Lieutenant. During his occupation of the country the Penal Laws were introduced which saw the confiscation of much more Catholic land:

"Under the post-Civil War Commonwealth regime most Irish Catholic landowners - whether Old Irish or Old English - were dispossessed of their land by law, some receiving smaller holdings in Connacht in recompense. After this point, Protestants owned the bulk of the land in Ireland."[33]

To this day, Irish Catholics, and the Irish diaspora, remember with opprobrium the name of Oliver Cromwell, not just for the confiscation of Catholic lands, but in particular for the brutal massacre of Catholics in Drogheda and Wexford on 11 September and 11 October 1649 respectively, evidence of which comes from his own report back to the speaker of the English parliament. The following harrowing description of these punitive incursions explains in some detail an important part of the historical background to English involvement in Ireland which led to such bitterness and resentment among the indigenous Irish:

"At the heart of Cromwell's conquest was the

[33] Richard English: Irish Freedom, p62

storming of Drogheda and Wexford. They represent a grim legend. In Drogheda more than three thousand were killed; in Wexford not less than 2,000. They died from artillery bombardment, from gunshots, from sword and dagger thrust, or by bludgeon – Sir Arthur Aston, commander of the Drogheda garrison, was beaten to death with his own wooden leg. Many, perhaps most, were killed in hot blood. But others were killed in cold blood after they had surrendered or been captured. Cromwell ordered none in military or religious orders to be spared."[34]

The actions of Cromwell in Drogheda and Wexford were seen by many as just reprisal for the events of 1641 and for the persecution of Protestants in Europe. Besides, it was argued, the granting of Irish land to the incoming settlers was necessary if the Plantation policy was to be successful. The truth is that apart from Ulster the policy had very limited success. Plantation neither subdued the Irish politically nor persuaded them to abandon Catholicism and the resentment caused by the policy simply encouraged incipient Irish nationalism.

The Penal Laws

The coercive Penal Laws which were passed by a Protestant Parliament of Ireland determined to disenfranchise the Catholic majority of all political and economic power were described by the Dublin born, Anglo-Irish statesman, philosopher and Whig M.P. Edmund Burke as:

"a machine ...as well fitted for the oppression, impoverishment and degradation of a people, and the

---

[34] The Cromwell Association Website

debasement in them of human nature itself, as ever proceeded from the perverted ingenuity of man."

From 1607 Catholics were barred from holding public office or serving in the Irish Army. To participate in any form of Catholic worship made one liable to fines or imprisonment and for any priest brave enough to say mass or practice any of his priestly duties there were severe penalties, including death. Catholics were barred from voting, holding any public office, owning land, or travelling abroad for a Catholic education. It was a crime punishable with transportation to teach Catholicism and a capital offence to convert a Protestant to Catholicism. Catholic Churches were transferred to the Anglican Church of Ireland, intermarriage with a Protestant who had an estate in Ireland was prohibited, and any children of a mixed marriage had to be brought up in the Protestant faith.

The Penal Laws, as had the policy of Plantation and the distribution of Irish land to loyal subjects of previous English monarchs for services rendered, resulted in a simmering resentment among the Catholic majority population. This resentment inevitably resulted in frequent revolts and attacks on the Protestant settlers and ruling classes as a consequence of which the colonists came to fear, resent and indeed loathe the indigenous Catholic population. The British government's response to the Great Famine in the nineteenth century did nothing to assuage the bitter resentment of Catholics. Indeed, the government's apparent indifference to the great suffering and mounting death toll among the indigenous population made matters infinitely worse.

The Great Famine (An Gorta Mór)

When the potato blight *(Phtophthora Infestans)* struck Ireland in 1845 the result was a famine disaster worse than any visited on other European countries at the time. Indeed, the outcome in Ireland was such that the Irish famine can legitimately be said to have had much more savage consequences than any of the many famines suffered in recent years which have been so graphically described in the relief appeals which have come to be a regular feature on our T.V. screens.

To understand why Ireland was so catastrophically affected by the blight, one has to appreciate that more than half of the population of 8.5 million relied predominately on the potato as the mainstay of their diet and of those more than half again relied almost exclusively on the potato for survival. As is almost always the case when natural disasters strike, the poorest members of the population suffered most. Of course, the arrival of the blight on Irish shores cannot be attributed to British government policy. However, the totally inadequate response of the government in London to the desperate plight of the Irish population would only serve to further exacerbate the bitter feelings of injustice and resentment of the indigenous Irish and further fan the flames of Irish Nationalism.

After the failure in 1798 of the revolt against the connection with England by the United Irishmen - a group largely led by Protestant idealists such as Theobald Wolfe Tone and Lord Edward Fitzgerald - the avowed aim of which was to bring together Protestants, Catholics and Dissenters in opposition to English interference in Ireland, the British establishment took the opportunity to suppress the Irish parliament in Dublin and return decision-making to Westminster. In a statement which could have come straight from the pen of Niccolo Machiavelli, and which gives credence to the assertion by Scottish Nationalists today that the Parliament in Westminster cannot be trusted, Edward Cooke, Under Secretary for the military department in the Irish administration, wrote in 1799:

"By giving the Irish a hundred members in an Assembly of six hundred and fifty they will be impotent to operate upon that Assembly, but it will be invested with Irish assent to its authority ......The Union is the only means of preventing Ireland from becoming too great and too powerful."

William Ewart Gladstone, who served as Prime Minister of the United Kingdom for four terms over a period of 12 years, was scathing of the 1800 Act of Union declaring that:

"There is no blacker or fouler transaction in the history of man. We used the whole civil government of Ireland as an engine of wholesale corruption...we obtained that Union against the sense of every class of the Community, by wholesale bribery and unblushing intimidation"[35]

Nevertheless, with the passing of the Act, combatting the disastrous effects of the famine should have become the responsibility of the British Parliament. Unfortunately, and not for the first or last time, elements of the British political and religious establishments did not see it that way and, as a result, subsequent political decisions contributed greatly to the death by starvation or disease of one million Irish men, women and children and the mass migration of a further million or more, principally to North America,

---

[35] Tim Pat Coogan: 1916, The Easter Rising, p17

but also to Canada and cities in Britain such as Liverpool and Glasgow. This at a time when Britain was the wealthiest nation in the world and therefore financially in a position to mitigate the worst aspects of the famine.

The fact that the Whig government chose to adhere strictly to economic convictions in the face of the desperate plight of the Irish, led the British Historian, A.J.P. Taylor to the conclusion that Prime Minister Lord John Russell, Chancellor of the Exchequer Sir Charles Wood and Assistant Secretary to the Treasury Sir Charles Edward Trevelyan,

" *were gripped by the most horrible, and perhaps the most universal, of human maladies: the belief that principles and doctrines are more important than lives. They imagined that rules, invented by economists, were as "natural" as the potato blight.*"[36]

Taylor went on to characterise the laissez-faire policies of the Whig government as genocidal and, given that adherence to such doctrinaire policies resulted in countless thousands of deaths in Ireland, it is hard to dispute such an assertion.

This messianic belief in laissez-faire politics, which abhorred any interference in the market economy, was compounded by the conviction of several ministers that the famine was visited on Ireland by an all-knowing, all-wise and all-merciful God as a result of the moral laxity of the Irish people. We can only imagine the economic and human disaster which would be visited on the British people were present day Conservative ministers to apply the same logic during the current corona-virus pandemic. However, since Whig ministers during the famine years firmly

---

[36] A.J.P Taylor: Essays in English History, p74

believed that Ireland's problems arose from the moral defects in the Irish character, when Trevelyan asserted in his book, "The Irish Crisis(1848)", that the famine was *"the sharp but effective remedy by which the cure is likely to be affected",* he was simply echoing these sentiments. Their firm belief in the market economy, divine intervention and Irish immorality, allowed government ministers, officials and landowners to convince themselves of the rectitude of their approach to the famine and to shield themselves from the murderous consequences of their policies. From a purely Scottish point of view it is interesting to note that powerful members of the Central Board of Management for Highland relief in Scotland, influenced by the views of Trevelyan who *"regarded both the Irish and Highland Celts as profoundly racially inferior to Anglo-Saxons"[37],* began to use the same racially motivated argument that the Highlanders, who in 1847 were also enduring famine conditions, were both feckless and indolent and had to learn to support themselves.

In Ireland, whether you believe that there was malevolent intent behind government policies, as did John Mitchell, the son of a Northern Irish Presbyterian minister, who declared that:

"a million and a half of men, women and children were carefully, prudently and peacefully slain by the English government. That they died of hunger in the midst of abundance which their own hands created", or that there was no evil intent behind government policy but simply a blind adherence to dogmatic policies, the end result of British government policies was affliction on a grand scale for the native Irish.

---

[37] T.M. Devine The Scottish Clearances, p310

A country which supplied almost 80% of corn imports to Britain was denied access to that corn at a time when access to it would have gone a long way to mitigate the loss of the potato. The government refused to close the ports to the export of grain and cattle, failed to make the cost of tackling the grievous consequences of the famine a whole United Kingdom responsibility and decreed that Irish ratepayers (landlords and tenants) must meet the cost of relief to the destitute, which in many areas they were manifestly not in the position to do.

The Poor Law Statute of June 1847 decreed that the old and infirm, the sick, orphans and widows with two or more legitimate children, would be eligible for relief, with the local board of guardians having the final decision as to whether that relief should be administered in or out of the workhouse. Unemployed or destitute able-bodied men would also be eligible for relief but only in the workhouse. As there were never enough workhouses to accommodate the thousands of starving and destitute people the local guardians were authorised to provide outdoor relief but only in the form of food and only for a two-month period.

However, most devastating of all the provisions of the Poor Law Statute was the quarter acre law, the aim of which was to provide landlords with the legal right to clear from their holdings those poor smallholders who were in arrears with their rents. According to this particular provision no one with holdings above quarter of an acre was eligible for relief unless and until they gave up their holding above quarter of an acre which many small-holders refused to do, preferring starvation for themselves and their families rather than surrendering their holdings knowing that the inevitable consequence of doing so would be the subsequent demolition of their houses. As a result of this provision, in the five-year period between 1849 and 1854, approximately 50,000 families, or a quarter of a million people, were evicted from their homes, with only exile, disease or death on the horizon.

Famine Memorial, Custom House Quay, Dublin

Emigration was the alternative to the workhouse or death by starvation but a large proportion of those at greatest risk of premature death – the poorest labourers and their families - were patently unable to meet the cost of this option. Only a small number of landlords were prepared to, or were in a position to, meet the cost of assisted passages and the government's laissez-faire policies did not countenance state assisted emigration which, given the alternatives, might have reduced the murderous death toll in Ireland.

Not that the countries to which they fled from the ravages of the famine offered a life of comfort. Far from it. Wherever they went they were looked down upon by the local inhabitants as dirty, inferior individuals to be shunned, despised, regarded with suspicion and exploited by ruthless employers. They

144

mostly lived in conditions of extreme squalor in major cities like Glasgow, Liverpool, London and New York - the principal ports of arrival after often extremely dangerous sea journeys in aptly named 'coffin' ships.

Thomas Annan's excellent book, *Photographs of the Old Closes and Streets of Glasgow, 1868/1877* - which was brought to my attention by a relative researching family history - includes a photo of No. 136 Saltmarket, the close where my great-grandparents lived. This series of photos by Annan give the reader an idea of the type of accommodation on offer to desperate immigrants and their offspring by unscrupulous, rapacious landlords when they arrived in 19th century Glasgow. The area where my great-grandparents settled in Glasgow with so many of their countrymen, which was referred to as District 14, was bounded by Trongate, Saltmarket, Clyde Street and Stockwell Street and encompassed the Bridgegate (Briggait), Osborne Street and Chisolm Street.

The unspeakable squalor of living conditions in district 14 has been well documented. In 1845 the German Philosopher Friedrich Engels described the horrors of these conditions in the following terms:

"I have seen human degradation in some of its worst phases, both in England and abroad, but I can advisedly say, that I did not believe, until I visited the wynds of Glasgow, that so large amount of filth, crime, misery, and disease existed in one spot in any civilised country." [38]

In his excellent account of the conditions faced by the Irish immigrants in Glasgow, John Burrowes describes District 14 as *"Glasgow's very own Hell's*

---

[38] Friedrich Engels: Conditions of the Working Class in England in 1844

Kitchen...a human cesspit, a concentration camp of filth and disease"[39] while a Report commissioned by the Glasgow Philosophical Society, which was presented to members in 1889, provided even more graphic descriptions of the squalor endured by those who found a "home" in District 14 and many of the poorer areas of Glasgow.

No.46 Saltmarket, Glasgow

No.136 Saltmarket, Glasgow (where my great-grandparents lived)

The Report included the following extract from a harrowing account of a visit by one of the commissioners to a tenement block in the district:

"There is no provision for ventilation or light – a dark and unwholesome dungeon. Along the passage and there's two or three houses on either side making in all eight to a dozen dwellings on the landing. Knock at a door. You enter briskly but suddenly fall back. Is there anyone living here? Can human life sustain itself here? Do not draw back. You have your inspection to complete so get on with it. Well, what do you see? The floor is covered with men, women and children huddled up promiscuously in corners of the room on

[39] John Burrowes: Irish

tressed beds or no beds at all or in closet beds with doors which, where you enter, were carefully shut to exclude even a suspicion of fresh air, were such a thing possible here. Rags, scraps of blankets and old clothing, grey with dirt and crawling with vermin, are wound in frowsy coils around the limbs of little children and of grown-up men and women."[40]

Not that that such insanitary conditions were only to be found in Glasgow. Most receiving cities located immigrants in similar dwellings. An address by the Manchester Board of Health in 1799 referred to similar living conditions and warned the poor to:

"Be careful to avoid living in dark, damp and confined cellars; or in backstreets adjoining to privies, or heaps of offensive and corrupted matter; and to avoid overcrowding in small rooms."[41]

Wherever the Irish fleeing from the horrendous conditions in their homeland eventually found themselves, they were faced with similar, if not worse living conditions.

The Soup Kitchen Act

When in 1846 the potato crop failed, Lord John Russell who had succeeded Sir Robert Peel as British prime minister, decided that the way to tackle the problem was not to make cheap food available but rather to provide paid employment by resuming the public works programme in October 1846. The problem was that those starving people who were fortunate enough to survive the failure of the 1845 crop, were now so

---

[40] Ibid: p91
[41] E.P. Hennock: "Urban Sanitary Reform before Chadwick?", Economic History Review, Vol. X, No. 1, 1957, p 113

seriously weakened through lack of sustenance that they were no longer in the condition to carry out the hard, physical outdoor work demanded of them. Following a harsh winter, the government abandoned the public works programme in February 1847 and passed instead the "Soup Kitchen Act". The *"Act for the Temporary Relief of Destitute Persons in Ireland,"* responsibility for which was placed on the district commissioners in order to allow the government to maintain its non-intervention policy, was not even the brain-child of ministers - Quakers had already set up soup kitchens all over Ireland. While they lasted the kitchens were successful in alleviating the hunger endured by many families, particularly in the rural areas, distributing three million daily rations by July of 1847. However, the Act stated that this was a temporary measure and official kitchens were closed in August of the same year.

Unfortunately, whatever good came of the soup kitchens was undone in the minds of many Catholics by reports that in many places soup was only given to those who were prepared to give up their faith and become Protestant. *"Souperism"*, as this practice came to be called, forced starving families to choose between their faith and food. Those who chose to take the soup were ostracised by their peers and often physically abused and to this day are still referred to as *"soupers"* in some quarters. The famine years, and in particular *Black '47,* left a legacy of bitterness which further fanned the flames of Irish nationalism. However, there was growing recognition among the more enlightened landowners that an alternative to repeated revolts by the dispossessed had to be found to redress obvious injustices.

Irish Home Rule Movement

When, in 1800, the Act of Union between Ireland and England removed the legislative independence of the Irish parliament, which had been secured by the efforts of Henry Grattan - an Anglo-Irish Protestant politician - and the Patriot Movement, it also removed any hope of Irish initiated reforms which might have gone some way to reduce tensions between opposing religious factions. Often initiated by Irish Protestants, throughout the nineteenth century there were several attempts to redress Catholic grievances, not all of which were restricted to a purely constitutional approach to resolving injustices. Among those who opted for the physical force strand of Irish nationalism, Robert Emmet, who came from a wealthy Anglo-Irish Protestant family, paid with his life for his leading role in the abortive rebellion against British rule in 1803. Following the failed revolt, he was eventually captured, tried for treason and executed on 20 September of the same year.

Although initially against the use of force to bring about change, the *Young Irelanders* - a breakaway group from Daniel O'Connell's *Repeal Association* - were inspired by republican movements in America and Europe in 1848, a time when the Great Famine was still raging. They embarked on a revolutionary course of action which, having failed, led to the capture, trial and deportation to Van Dieman's Land, of nationalist leaders William Smith O'Brien - a Protestant landowner - and Thomas Francis Meagher.

The *Fenian Rising* of 5 March 1867 was no more successful. There were two strands to the Fenian movement. The Fenian Brotherhood was founded in the United States in 1858, the same year as the Irish

Republican Brotherhood (IRB) was founded in Dublin by James Stephen, a civil engineer. For the first time an Irish movement was able to appeal to the Irish community in America for financial support and military expertise and indeed, the military leaders of the Fenian Rising were Irish veterans who had fought on the side of the Union Army in the American Civil War.

Unfortunately for the IRB, the British authorities were forewarned of the rising by the informer John Joseph Croydon, one of Stephens' trusted agents, and this betrayal plus poor organisation led to the revolt being quickly suppressed. However, the Fenians' proclamation of a Provisional Republican government did resonate with many Irishmen both in Ireland and America as it listed the grievances which had led to the rising and the previous failed efforts to address them through appeals to reason. If there was ever to be a peaceful resolution to the growing sectarian tensions in Ireland, natural justice required that long held grievances could not forever be ignored:

The Irish People of the World,

We have suffered centuries of outrage, enforced poverty, and bitter misery. Our rights and liberties have been trampled on by an alien aristocracy, who treating us as foes, usurped our lands, and drew away from our unfortunate country all material riches. The real owners of the soil were removed to make room for cattle and driven across the ocean to seek the means of living, and the political rights denied to them at home, while our men of thought and action were condemned to loss of life and liberty. But we never lost the memory and hope of a national existence, we appealed in vain to the reason and sense of justice of the dominant

*powers. Our mildest remonstrances were met with
sneers and contempt. Our appeals to arms were always
unsuccessful. Today, having no honourable alternative
left, we again appeal to force as our last resort.*

Daniel O'Connell, Irish politician and champion of
Catholic rights, referred to by King George IV as the
"uncrowned King of Ireland", successfully fought for
and secured Catholic Emancipation in 1829, but,
despite repeated efforts by the Association to repeal the
Act of Union he died before realising his dream. In the
fifty years from the 1870s it fell to the Home Rule
movement to take on the task and to seek by
constitutional means the repeal of the Act.

Born in County Donegal, son of a Church of Ireland
rector, Isaac Butt, barrister and MP, concluded that the
only way to curtail the frequent risings against
parliament in Westminster was to argue for a federal
system which would allow the Irish themselves to
address the problem of inefficient administration on
the island. In 1870 he founded the Irish Home
Government Association with the idea of gathering
support for an Irish parliament with control over
domestic matters. This was quickly replaced in 1873
with the Home Rule League which in 1874 returned
sixty members to parliament in Westminster.

In 1882 the League was in turn replaced by the Irish
Parliamentary Party, which under the more forceful
Charles Stewart Parnell, an Anglo-Irish Protestant
landowner, embarked on an obstructionist campaign in
Westminster which came close to realising the dream
of Home Rulers when the Liberal government of
William Ewart Gladstone introduced the First Home
Rule Bill in 1886. Unfortunately, and not for the last
time, Conservative opposition to a resolution to the

Irish problem for their own political gain, came in the form of support for Ulster Unionists' *'right to fight'* against the imposition of Home Rule. The British Conservative, Lord Randolph Churchill, at a meeting in Belfast went as far as to assert that the Unionists could count on the support of people in high places in the British establishment should they indeed choose to *'fight.'*

Tim Pat Coogans in his book "1916: The Easter Rising", highlighted the glaring contradictions in the Unionist opposition to Home Rule:

"The meeting held on 22 February 1886 in the Ulster hall had been advertised in the Belfast Newsletter as a 'conservative demonstration – a monster meeting of Conservative and Orangemen'. Churchill's presence and the commitments he made thus gave a benison to a remarkable feature of the Orange philosophy – its ability to preach 'loyalty', constitutionalism and religious liberty while at the same time either threatening or practising treason, violence, the arousal of sectarian hatred and the denial of human rights."[42]

As a consequence of Conservative opposition and a split within the Liberal Party the First Home Rule bill was defeated in the House of Commons and another opportunity for a possible eventual peaceful resolution to the Irish problem was lost. Following the defeat of the bill, Gladstone resigned, as the Conservatives had calculated he would after such a setback and was replaced by the Tory leader Lord Salisbury. However, Gladstone was returned to office following his victory at the 1892 General Election and immediately proceeded to prepare a second Home Rule bill which

---

[42] Tim Pat Coogans: 1916: The Easter Rising (p7)

was put before Parliament in February 1893. This time the bill passed the House of Commons hurdle only to be defeated by the Conservative controlled House of Lords, highlighting once more the gulf between Liberals and Conservatives in their approach to the Irish question.

The stand-off between Liberals and Conservatives over Home Rule for Ireland continued into the twentieth century and came to a head once again when, on 11 April 1912, a Third Home Rule Bill was moved in the House of Commons by the Liberal Prime Minister, Henry Asquith. Even before this first reading of the Bill, Andrew Bonar Law, the leader of the Conservative opposition, had expressed in the strongest possible terms his support for opposition to Home Rule at a mass demonstration in Balmoral, a suburb of Belfast - a demonstration which further strengthened the close relationship between Ulster Protestantism and the Conservative and Unionist Party. He followed up this intervention at Balmoral with a speech at Blenheim Palace, in July 1912, which amounted to an incitement to rebellion in order to block Home Rule. He declared that Ulster would be justified in using force to this end if necessary:

"I can imagine no length of resistance to which Ulster can go in which I should not be prepared to support them."

He was playing a dangerous game but one which was calculated to gain the support of the more extreme elements in the Tory Party, in order to bolster his own precarious position, and to create a parliamentary impasse over Home Rule in order to force a general election and the return of the Conservatives to power. Once again the Conservatives were playing the Orange Card for their own political ends without regard to the long-term consequences for ordinary people, not only of Ulster but of the whole of Ireland.

No doubt emboldened by the support of the leader of the Conservative Party, as well as of senior members of the British establishment, and given their absolute determination to block government from Dublin, on 13 December, 1912, members of the Ulster Unionist Council agreed to the creation of a paramilitary force to defeat Home Rule for Ireland. The Ulster Volunteer Force was established in January of the following year and, by 1914, counted almost 100,000 volunteers in its ranks. A response to the formation of the UVF from nationalists was only to be expected and in January 1913 the Irish Volunteer Force was formed with the aim of securing and maintaining *"the rights and the liberties common to the whole people of Ireland."* By mid-1914 the nationalist force had strengthened to almost 200,000 volunteers. Interestingly, the British government reacted to the formation of the Irish Volunteer Force by introducing a ban on the import of arms, something which it had singularly failed to do following the formation of the UVF.

The Curragh Mutiny

When it became known that discussions had taken place within the Liberal government about the use of the army to confront the UVF, the Commander-in-Chief in Ireland, General Sir Arthur Paget, on 20 March, 1914, informed the War Office that General Hubert Gough and fifty-seven officers of the Third Cavalry Brigade stationed in Curragh, County Clare, had indicated that they preferred dismissal to moving against the UVF in Ulster. This threatened refusal to take action against the drilling UVF was reinforced by

Bonar Law, the leader of His Majesty's Loyal Opposition, who *"informed King George V that he would advise British Army officers to refuse any orders that directed them to take action against Ulster."* (1916: The Easter Rising, p.56) No doubt encouraged by this turn of events, a mere month later, on the night of 24-25 April an illegal shipment of 25,000 rifles and three million rounds of ammunition for use by the UVF was landed secretly and unimpeded - mainly in Larne - by a British Army officer, Major Fred Crawford, who so opposed the idea of Home Rule that he openly professed that he would prefer to change his allegiance to the German Emperor rather than be ruled from Dublin – this on the eve of a threatened war with Germany.

As a result of the Curragh mutiny and support for the UVF by certain members of the Conservative Party, including the Party leader, as well as the import of arms for the UVF, many Irish people simply did not believe that the British Army could be relied upon to enforce the Home Rule Bill which was passed by the House of Commons on 25 May, 1914 by a majority of 77 votes. There was an inevitability about the response from the nationalist Irish Volunteers. Ironically, and not for the first time during the growth of nationalism in Ireland, while the Protestant UVF was arming for opposition to Home Rule, among those who responded immediately to this unconstitutional threat were prominent Protestant nationalists.

The group of wealthy British and Anglo-Irish Church of Ireland supporters of Home Rule who formed a committee in London to raise funds for the purchase of arms for the Irish Volunteers included Sir Roger Casement, Erskine Childers, Mary Childers, Mary Spring Rice, Darrel Figgis and Alice Stopford

Rice. They not only funded the purchase of 1,500 rifles and 49,000 rounds of ammunition but Erskine and Molly Childers used their yacht, the *Asgar,* to land 900 rifles and 29,000 rounds of ammunition in Howth, County Dublin, on 26 July 1914. The *Kelpie*, the smaller of the two yachts to rendezvous with the German tug-boat Gladiator took on board 600 rifles and 20,000 rounds of ammunition which were subsequently transferred to the engine-powered *Chotah* skippered by Sir Thomas Myles, another Church of Ireland supporter of Home Rule and a former President of the Royal College of Surgeons. Off the coast of Dublin, the *Chotah's* cargo was transferred to the fishing boat, the *Nugget*, on 1 August, and landed at Kilcoole, County Wicklow, less than a week after the Howth landing and three days before Britain declared war on Germany.

With the outbreak of the First World War implementation of Home Rule was suspended and John Edward Redmond, who had succeeded Parnell as leader of the Irish Parliamentary Party, called on the Irish Volunteers to join Irish regiments of the British Army. He believed that this would ensure implementation of Home Rule after a war which was expected to be of short duration. However, the Army's refusal to respond to UVF manoeuvres and the inclusion in Asquith's coalition government formed in May 1915 of those who had openly advocated what amounted to treasonous opposition to government policy on Home rule proved too much for Nationalists – Bonar Law was rewarded with the position of Secretary of State for the Colonies while Sir Edward Carson became Attorney-General with a seat in Cabinet. Not surprisingly, Redmond's call to arms in support of the British war effort proved fatal for the

IPP and resulted in a split in the Volunteers some of whom went on to participate in the unsuccessful rising against British rule in 1916. The arrest and subsequent execution of the leaders of the Easter Rising resulted in a radical shift in public opinion away from the Home Rule movement to the more militant republican Sinn Féin Party with the result that, in the 1918 election, the Irish Parliamentary Party was decimated and the Home Rule movement was effectively dead.

The great gulf between the Nationalist and Unionist communities in Ireland was further exacerbated by the ferocious conduct of the Irish War of Independence (1919-1921). It was an unequal struggle in which the Irish Republican Army faced the combined forces of the British Army, the Royal Irish Constabulary bolstered by the *Black and Tans*, the paramilitary *Auxiliaries* and the Ulster Special Constabulary which included the remnants of the UVF and therefore a Protestant force in the eyes of Nationalists. The Anglo-Irish Treaty, (6 December, 1921) which ended that war was the signal for a Civil War between those nationalists who supported the Treaty and those who were determined to free the whole of Ireland from British Rule – the Government of Ireland Act of 1920 had given Northern Ireland the option of opting out of the Free State and remaining part of Britain. The Treaty sanctioned a Northern Ireland, not of the nine counties of Ulster as Carson, supported by Bonar Law, had argued for in his New Year's Day, 1913, amendment to the Home Rule Bill, but of the six counties with Unionist majorities. Unfortunately for the signatories the compromise arrived at in the Treaty failed to solve the problem of how to satisfy the wildly different aspirations of the two communities and so the problem has continued into a new millennium.

Chapter 14

Truth, Myth and Fake News

"The most brilliant propaganda technique will yield no success unless one fundamental principal is borne in mind constantly – it must confine itself to a few points and repeat them over and over."

Joseph Goebbels

In our discussions concerning the ever present problem of the *Us* and *Them* mentality so prevalent world-wide, while always recognising the fundamental importance of education, neither Luis nor I were under any illusions about the many obstacles to the implementation of a successful strategy to combat hateful divisions and to promote peaceful coexistence. Having dedicated so many years of his life to his work in UNESCO Luis, as well as anyone, recognises the difficulty of overcoming the distrust engendered by historical injustices, the need to help people better understand when they are being used, to see through the rhetoric of populists and to recognise the difference between truth, fake news and myth.

The electoral success of Boris Johnson's ad nauseum repetition of the mantra "Let's get Brexit done" and Donald Trump's promise to "Make America Great Again" are two of the most recent examples of the efficacy of the advice regarding propaganda offered by Joseph Goebbels, Hitler's Propaganda Minister. In terms of the historical situation in Ireland, the constantly repeated claim that Home Rule would lead to Rome Rule was equally successful in persuading the Protestant population of Ulster to oppose the Home Rule Bill, with violence if necessary. Words have all the significance of weapons to the ignorant mind and people in positions of power have a responsibility to temper their language when attacking opponents or seeking support. Unfortunately, there is a growing number of dangerous populists only too willing to exploit the ignorance and fears of people in order to secure themselves in power, irrespective of the inevitable social and political consequences of their actions.

Donald Trump and Jair Bolsonaro are two such populists who were democratically elected to the highest Office in their respective countries. Before his defeat in the 2020 election, Donald Trump strutted about the American stage like a modern-day Caligula, displaying all the arrogance of a Mussolini, constantly whipping up his followers with the language of an uneducated lout, telling them they were *'lucky to have him as President'.* His refusal to accept the result of the 2020 election, his persistent claims that the election was stolen by voter fraud, and his call to his supporters to march on the Capitol Building in Washington led inevitably to the death and destruction which followed. His clone Jair Bolsonaro, President of Brazil, is another cut from the same cloth. He too foments hatred against minorities often speaking out against black and indigenous people and homosexuals, using language which has created a climate of fear, especially among the nation's black population who make up about half of the nation's people:

"Racism in Brazil, whether it is political intimidation from the President, bullets from paramilitary forces and now, Covid-19, makes a target

of black people across Brazil."[43]

Fully aware of the prejudices of those who make up their support base, too often politicians use those sections of the media which are sympathetic to their stated policies as a platform to demonize opponents - minority groups are convenient scapegoats when it is necessary to divert public attention from the detrimental effects of particularly socially divisive policies. Unfortunately, there are those who too readily believe that:

"When you have a thing in print – in black and white – why there it is, and you can't get away from it! If it wasn't alright, a paper like that would never have printed it."[44]

Of course, those reporters, newspapers and TV channels prepared to question the underlying motivation of certain government policies, or indeed the veracity of some of the statements put out by leaders or government officials, are often ignored, given short shrift or worse. Trump's attacks on the press are well documented and according to the National Federation of Journalists, violence against press workers increased by 54% in Brazil in the year after Bolsonaro's election in 2018.

Unfortunately, too many people in the West are blind to what goes on in their own country. They have come to believe that these tendencies are confined to authoritarian regimes or military dictatorships. Not so.

"The election of Mr Trump demonstrated that democracies are not immune to the cult of personality and the attraction of a strong man with easy answers

[43] Bianca Santana: Guardian, 22 June 2020
[44] Robert Tressell: The Ragged Trousered Philanthropists, p.102

to hard questions."[45]

Populist politicians and parties, which threaten to weaken and erode democracy as we know it, are springing up all over Europe and the Trump era in the United States – the country which is most often held up as a beacon of democracy – is a cause for great concern, not only for many U.S citizens but for people throughout the world. Attacks on the free press are particularly worrying as Douglas Brinkley, historian at Rice University, points out:

"We're now moving through dangerous waters. A fundamental part of authoritarianism is stifling the free press. If he (Trump) succeeds in turning the press into 'false news' and 'the enemy of the people' he will succeed in eliminating the main obstacle for an authoritarian government."[i46]

If the mantra 'fake news' is repeated often enough when applied to press criticism of governmental policy, and reporters can be labelled 'enemies of the people', how are politicians and governments to be held to account?

Immigrants have always been favourite targets for populists who know only too well that vulnerable sections of society are particularly receptive to any policy which advocates 'keeping immigrants out' or 'sending them back.' How often do we hear criticism of immigrants in the pubs and working-men's clubs here in Britain, especially in times of crisis, and from the mouth of people who themselves are very frequently descendants of immigrants. I have at times had occasion to remind friends in my own local that most of the pub's patrons are but a generation or two

---

[45] Tim Marshall: Prisoners of Geography, p.89
[46] Jim Acosta: El Enemigo del Pueblo, p392

removed from their immigrant parents or grandparents. Most often the complaint is that *They* take *Our* homes, *Our* jobs and *Our* children's school places or that *They* are spongers who contribute little to society, that their availability in the job market drives down wages, and indeed that many are criminals. In the U.S, when he came to power Donald Trump labelled Mexican immigrants as rapists and delinquents, and his presidential decree of 29th January 2019 banned entry to the U.S of anyone from seven predominantly Muslim countries. He constantly plays on the fears and prejudices of his supporters about supposed enemies, whether internal or external, and the threat they pose to the security of the country, assuring his base support that he and not tolerance would protect them. During his presidency he was frequently responsible for interventions which sowed the seeds of hatred, division and violence - a deliberate tactic which served him well at the polls but which also alienated millions of American citizens

His assertions about immigrants, like many of those echoed in certain sections of the British media, are frequently untrue, and simply reinforce the prejudices of those who hear what they want to hear, see what they want to see and believe what they have been conditioned to believe. There is often no attempt to verify the truth of the immigrants' real contribution to our society; no attempt to inform people about the necessity of attracting inward immigration to countries, especially in Europe, where there is a crisis of ageing populations; no criticism made of those employers who exploit the immigrants in order to keep wages down; no mention of the fact that many employers find it difficult to attract British workers to do many of the jobs done by immigrants - farmers in particular are predicting the loss of many crops due to the absence of immigrant workers at this time of the corona virus pandemic; and no criticism made of the government's failure to build houses. The problem is that *"a lie told once remains a lie, but a lie told a thousand times becomes the truth"* (Joseph Goebbels). It cannot be repeated often enough that unscrupulous politicians and leaders too often reinforce the prejudices of people in order to better exploit those prejudices for their own advantage.

Much more serious than the verbal abuse of those who are in some way different, however, is the all too frequent resort to violence and intimidation against those who do not share the majority view as to how life should be lived. The more deep-rooted the belief that *We* hold the key to humanity's salvation and that *They* are resistant to, or indeed threaten *Our* way of life, the greater the hatred of *Them*. Extreme examples of the result of such hatred can be seen in the present day persecution of the Rohingya people in Myanmar (Burma), the detention and reported ill-treatment of Uyghurs in 're-education' camps in China and the genocide of the Yazidis by the Islamic State.

Unfortunately, the careless and divisive rhetoric of some in positions of power which gives oxygen to that hatred, results in a growing number of race attacks throughout the world whether by Islamist, far-right, religious, political or sectarian extremists, and helps to perpetuate existing systemic racism in the very institutions which are supposed to protect vulnerable citizens irrespective of race colour or creed.

Myths

When I was only twelve or thirteen years old and in

Canniesburn Hospital recovering from an appendectomy which had been performed in Glasgow Royal Infirmary, I was recuperating in a ward with a man in his forties who was hearing impaired and unable to speak. He and I became very friendly, principally because I was one of the few people who found it easy to communicate with him. I had no knowledge of sign language but by spelling out words on our hands we were able to hold simple conversations. When members of the nursing staff wanted to pass on instructions to him, they would inevitably come to me to help relay the message. He was a simple, uneducated Irishman and what I most remember about him was that he frequently woke up in the middle of the night, wild-eyed and screaming in terror. Staff would often come to me, as someone he trusted, to help calm him down. After several such episodes I eventually managed to persuade him to reveal the source of his fears. He was subject to recurrent nightmares about the *Banshee* coming for him. From stories passed down from my Irish grandparents I knew that the *Banshee*, a female spirit in Irish mythology, was a harbinger of death. He was terrified.

It would be easy to scoff at his ignorance and his naivety, and to take his fears to be those of a psychologically immature adult, but the truth is that the Banshee as a symbol of death has her counterpart in other cultures – in the Christian tradition the *White Horse* is another example of a symbol used as a portent of impending death and is frequently used in literature for that purpose. Myths and symbols constantly repeated over the centuries can pass into the psyche of a people. In the struggle between Good and Evil, the apparent human need for heroes, has been depicted down through the centuries in *Hero Myths*, whether from the mythology of Greece and Rome, the Middle Ages, the Far East or from the primitive tribes of Africa and the Americas. Today these mythological heroes have their counterparts in comic heroes such as Superman, Batman or Captain America who like the heroes of the past inevitably triumph over evil adversaries.

Whether in oral tradition or written form, the truth is that humans down through the ages have forever been influenced by stories which recount past personal or group experiences, real or apocryphal, historical events or myths. The latter, in particular, have played a fundamental role in shaping society and social behaviour. Indeed, Mircea Eliade, historian of religion, philosopher, and professor at the University of Chicago, argued that one of the principal functions of myths is to establish models for behaviour. Of course, the main characters of myths are normally gods or supernatural beings and rulers have used this to their advantage throughout history. Alexander the Great declared himself a God as did the Pharaohs of Egypt and the Shahs of Persia. Even Cleopatra doubled as a god-queen. James VI of Scotland, as James I of England, in a speech to Parliament in 1610 went as far as to declare that:

"The state of monarchy is the supremist thing upon earth, for kings are not only God's lieutenants upon earth and sit upon God's throne, but even by God himself they are called Gods."

Nor need we reach so far back in time for evidence of this deification of rulers. It was not until the end of World War II, when state support for the Shinto religion was abolished, that the idea of the Emperor of Japan as direct descendant of the gods was dismissed.

One of the last acts of Emperor Hirohito was to issue an imperial rescript - the Humanity Declaration - as part of a New Year statement on 1 January 1946, towards the end of which he denied the concept of his being a living God:

"The ties between Us and Our people have always stood upon mutual trust and affection. They do not depend upon mere legends and myths. They are not predicated on the false conception that the Emperor is divine, and that the Japanese people are superior to other races and fated to rule the world."

So, stories real or fabricated, legends or myths, have always been used by rulers and strong men as a means of consolidating their power and exerting social control. For a perfect present-day example of the latter, one only has to consider the situation in North Korea where the 'Supreme Leader', Kim Jong-un is quasi-deified by millions. Whether induced by fear or genuine reverence, the scenes of apparently adoring crowds cheering their leader is difficult for people in the developed world to comprehend. Now, into the 21st century, most people, certainly in democratic countries, are not so naïve as to be taken in by what they consider to be absurd claims of deification of rulers or the need to placate angry gods with sacrifices.

The truth is that technology is now a much more effective way of controlling the populace, as any journey on public transport will show. During my short, weekly train trips to Glasgow from Airdrie, inevitably eight out of ten passengers will be sitting with their eyes firmly glued to their smart phones, totally oblivious to all around them and blissfully unaware of the fact that, far from them controlling technology, technology is controlling them. The majority of people seem oblivious to the fact that many of the big data driven surveillance algorithms are constantly surveying individuals in the service of major corporations and governments although even more worryingly some seem to accept the fact with equanimity.

The scope of the information gathered by these data-collecting companies was recently highlighted by Leo Kelion, BBC News's Technology desk editor, who submitted a data subject access request asking Amazon to disclose everything it knows about him. What came back was very revealing. One database contained transcriptions of 31,082 interactions which he and his family had had with the virtual assistant Alexa. Amazon was able to inform him that 2,670 product searches had been made within its store since 2017. Files were able to reveal not only which devices were used but also how many times they were used and from which location. Every customer interaction provides the opportunity to collect more data. The truth is:

"We are living in the era of hacking humans. The algorithms are watching you right now."[47]

In October 2019 the New York Times published an open letter to Mark Zuckerberg and other leaders of Facebook signed by hundreds of employees decrying the company's decision to let politicians post any claims they wanted – even false ones – in ads on the site. While praising the fact that the platform provided the opportunity for people to express their views, and to debate and share opinions, the letter raised concerns about the policy which allows politicians to:

"weaponize our platform by targeting people who believe that content posted by political figures is

---

[47] Yucal Noah Harari: 21 Lessons for the 21st Century, p311

trustworthy…. allowing paid civic misinformation to run on the platform…communicates that we are O.K. profiting from deliberate misinformation campaigns by those in, or seeking, positions of power."[48]

No doubt the employees had in mind what happened during the 2016 U.S elections when unofficial Russian intelligence apparatus used the enormous power of Facebook to disseminate misleading information in order to demobilise the Democratic vote in key states.

Sam Wineburg, professor of Education and History at the University of Stanford in California, who has studied the credibility that the public give to information on the internet, carried out a study in 2016 to ascertain whether young people were able to distinguish between real and misleading information and false news which appear on the internet. The results were disheartening. The majority of the young people were unable to distinguish between an advert and a piece of news and readily believed statements on social networks without making any attempt at verification. Jonathan Sumption in his bestseller "Trials of the State" highlights the root of the problem:

"Social media encourage a resort to easy answers and generate a powerful herd instinct which suppresses not just dissent but doubt and nuance as well." [49]

There was a time when I believed that social media might offer an alternative to some of the more blatant, politically biased press reports in Britain. In fact, what social media has done has been to give a platform to people who have had no hesitation in using the internet

---

[48] The New York Times, 28th October 2019
[49] Jonathan Sumption: Trials of the State

to disseminate lies and half-truths and who are prepared to use the vilest, totally unacceptable language to attack and intimidate opponents, often while hiding behind a cloak of anonymity. It is disheartening to witness the abuse of social media by often illiterate trolls and to hear the press being labelled as *the 'enemy of the people'* by Donald Trump for having the temerity to question some of his most divisive policies, as well as the veracity of the contents of many of his tweets. Another cause for concern to me was the avoidance of incisive press scrutiny by Boris Johnston during the period up to the 2020 General Election in the United Kingdom. The treatment of the press by Trump and Johnston have reinforced my firm belief in the importance of courageous, unbiased investigative journalists, who are able to distinguish between truth and the spin and machinations of vested interests. The world needs independent, not embedded, journalists and an education system which produces an electorate which can recognise the difference.

Education

As former teachers, most of the conversations between Luis and I invariably return to the subject of education and a recognition of the fact that in this digital world of half-truths, lies, false news, innuendo and human hacking it has never been more important for people to look beyond the headlines, not to accept things at face value or without evidence, to be able to make sense of information, to be able to tell the difference between what is important and what is unimportant, and above all to be able to distinguish between factual information and false news. According to a recent piece by Daniel Finkelstein, journalist and politician,

"This was the decade when we began to open our eyes to the truth. We are less ignorant, less deferential, more sceptical. We appreciate better how easy it is to say something untrue in politics and get away with it. We challenge more."[50]

I have no doubt that in the educated circles in which the reporter moves there is now a greater understanding of the threat to truth in politics. However, I am afraid that it is far from being universally true. There are still too many politicians and people in power who are of the opinion that truth should almost never be spoken as it only brings grief, sadness and destruction insisting that:

"Truth is fine in mathematics, chemistry and philosophy. Not in life. In life illusion, imagination, desire and hope are more important"[51]

Certainly, being economical with the truth in no way hindered the progress of Donald Trump to the Presidency of the United States or Boris Johnston to an overwhelming electoral triumph in the U.K. The most powerful enemy of truth is ignorance and, as has already been pointed out, social media interventions too often encourage a resort to easy answers to complex questions. Unfortunately, most people don't have the time, the inclination or indeed the political interest to read beyond misleading headlines or tweets, many of which are deliberately designed to tap into existing fears and prejudices for political ends.

I make no apologies for returning to the recurring theme in our conversations – the importance of education. Throughout my teaching career I was never comfortable with the way the school curriculum was

---

[50] Daniel Finkelstein: The Times 1st January, 2020
[51] Ernesto Sábato: Sobre Héroes y Tumbas, pp128/129

delivered and in particular the emphasis placed on the importance of preparing pupils for exams and the employment market. A school's reputation was, and indeed still is, dependant on exam results, which determine the school's ranking in published league tables, and not on turning out well-rounded individuals capable of independent thinking. This emphasis on the importance of results in academic subjects puts pressure on staff to teach towards exams to the detriment of a more rounded education and, all too often, to the detriment of less academic pupils. Subjects are often chosen on the basis that they are prerequisites for particular, mostly professional, jobs or for entry qualifications to college or university. Important as exams and job prospects are, unfortunately other important subjects which would enrich a pupil's education and life experience are rejected because they are not deemed to enhance career advancement.

In order to enable people to rise above petty squabbles and blind hatred of the *Other*, to understand the nature and purpose of myths, to get beyond headlines as well as the rhetoric of populists, and to understand the difference between truth and fake news, an emphasis on critical thinking in all educational establishments is of paramount importance. Pupils and students must be prepared to question everything which affects their world and their daily lives. Nothing should be taken at face value or accepted without evidence. If friction between communities or countries is to be overcome, we all of us have to try to better understand the way of life, the beliefs, the fears and the cultural background of the *Other*. In a world of 7.7 billion people living on a planet which Carl Sagan referred to as the 'Pale Blue Dot' in the universe, there is never going to be a uniform acceptance of one set of religious beliefs, of one particular political doctrine or one way of life – God protect us from those who are so full of their own self-importance that they must be masters of their own little corner of this mere 'dot' in the cosmos. As has already been established, major problems arise when fundamentalists, in their imagined self-importance, insist on imposing their way of life on others. If peoples are to co-exist, we have to find the best way to accommodate differences and this can only be done through communication. Students must be made aware that:

"Dialogue, which opens the way to understanding, is radically opposed to confrontation and wars: stupidity, arrogance and covetousness on the other hand get in the way of and impede understanding..... the message is clear: understanding of the 'Others' point of view or culture is the way to rapprochement and a recognition of the human need for such an understanding in order to be able to co-exist in peace."[52]

Of course, as well as critical thinking and the importance of dialogue, a genuine concern for the well-being of others less fortunate is another prerequisite for peaceful co-existence. Injustice, oppression and grinding poverty lead inevitably to social unrest. When humankind fails to learn the lessons of history, the carnage, horror and futility of past wars are inevitably repeated, as witness the thousands of refugees at present fleeing wars in the Middle East and Africa. When powerful countries, or powerful groups within a country, seek to expand their

---

[52] Miguel León-Portilla, antropólogo: la comprensión del otro, El País, 13 Septiembre 2004

influence by imposition rather than persuasion, the result is a festering sense of resentment and injustice among those they seek to dominate, those who are inevitably relegated to the status of second-class citizens in their own land, ignored and left behind.

Nature has a way of reminding us at times that we humans are social beings and therefore interdependent. The contagious Corona Virus now sweeping the world is a timely reminder that we are all vulnerable to disease and, without exception, bound to be affected by the present outbreak, either directly or indirectly. Unlike the virus of hatred spread against the *'Other'* by those who feel the need to demonstrate their own, their sect's or their nation's perceived superiority, Covid-19 is not selective in its choice of victims. It is neither racist nor sectarian. Nor does it respect social status – as Donald Trump and Boris Johnston discovered. It makes no distinction between races or creeds, between Brexiteers or Remainers, between Capitalists or Socialists. It attacks Us and Them in equal measure. On a hospital bed, dependant on a ventilator, only a fool would insist on knowing the racial, religious, or political background of the doctors and nurses striving to keep him/her alive at considerable personal risk to themselves. One would hope that once the present crisis is over, the example of the dedication and the sacrifices made by medical staff and front-line workers of all races and beliefs as well as the generosity of ordinary people, would have taught us all the value of co-operation and compassion. If not, the purveyors of bigotry, racism, fear and suspicion of *Them* will quickly find their voice again. We cannot deny or ignore the existence of human depravity and ignorance, *"perversi difficile corriguntur et stultorum infinitus est numerus."*

(Ecclesiastes 1:15)

While it is true that it is difficult for truly evil people to change their ways and ignorance and stupidity abound in the world, my hope and indeed confidence rests with our young people. Just as they have woken up to the existential threat of climate change I see in many of them a tolerance of differences in colour or creed which puts their elders to shame. Those of us who have witnessed or experienced intolerance in our lifetime mustn't ignore the fact that it continues to rear its ugly head or that it is a constant in our societies - *"The only thing necessary for the triumph of evil is for good men to do nothing." (Edmund Burke)*

But how can we best confront and challenge the cancer of ignorance and intolerance? How can we best combat and overcome the triple threat from populism, nativism and demagoguery? How can we best persuade people not to blindly accept simple answers to complex problems? The answer, of course, lies with an education system which does more than prepare people for the labour market. Equally important is the need to highlight and promote the need for an understanding and appreciation of differences between people, whether due to culture, race, religion or politics. If the present covid-19 pandemic has taught us anything it is that we are all vulnerable to a greater or lesser degree, no matter our creed or colour, and that if we are to overcome the virus we, all of us, have to play our part. The same can be said for the struggle against the virus of hatred and disdain of the *Other*.

Politicians are in a position to set an example of understanding, tolerance and compassion and people like Luis Ignacio Ramallo Massanet who work for organisations like UNESCO which directly challenge the cancer of hatred and ignorance are in the forefront of the struggle to bring about change in attitudes. Of course, we cannot all be politicians. Nor are we all involved in organisation like UNESCO, U.N., OXFAM or Médecins Sans Frontières. However, we can all support those directly involved in the struggle for a more just, equitable and compassionate society and in a democracy, by ensuring that we exercise our right to use our vote in elections, we can hold our politicians to account when self-interest comes before their responsibilities to constituents.

The very least we can do is to challenge those with whom we come in contact when they mimic anti-immigrant vitriol, repeating endlessly unsubstantiated, and indeed blatantly untrue and scurrilous allegations against people they have made no effort to understand. History is littered with examples of how unscrupulous individuals have taken advantage of differences of race, creed or colour for their own advantage and with frequently disastrous consequences. However, before we can challenge others, we all of us need to look in the mirror. Even good men and women have their prejudices. If we are better to understand others, it is essential that we first be honest with ourselves. It takes courage to admit to our own prejudices and weaknesses. It takes even more courage to publicly confront aggressive life-long bigots. Unfortunately, good men and women are not by nature heroes. Challenging our own prejudices is neither easy nor convenient. Most people are wary about involving themselves in actions or confrontations which might disturb their own normally quiet, peaceful lives. 'If it was just me, but I have to think of the possible repercussions for my family or my job,' they say. Many good men and women have justified their inaction in the face of injustice for this very reason and so the very racist attitudes they privately condemn and strongly disapprove of continue to go unchallenged. Given that by nature my preference is to avoid confrontation, faced with the problem of challenging racists or bigots I frequently have to remind myself of Ariel Dorfman's dictum:

"Do not cry tomorrow for what you did not have the courage and the wisdom to defend today."[53]

It has been my experience in a long life that silence is almost always interpreted by racists as an acceptance of their views.

The recent killing of a black man, George Floyd, in Minneapolis by a white policeman is the most recent example of what happens when racism is not confronted by society, another example of the cancer of the Us and Them mentality, another example of the arrogance of people who see themselves as superior beings to their victims. The reaction throughout the world to this, the latest death of a black man at the hands of the police in America, has been encouraging and has forced authorities here in Britain, for example, to consider how best to respond to the protests organised by 'Black Lives Matter' campaigners. Governments, while rightly condemning the violent and unjustifiable behaviour of a minority of protesters, must not be distracted from the real issue. We have been here before. There have been numerous reports published, purportedly aimed at tackling the issue of racial inequality and injustice in Britain. We have had the McPherson Report, the Lammy Report, the Windrush and Angeline Reports, and the Grenfell Inquiry and yet recent protests have highlighted the

---

[53] Ariel Dorfman: Emeritus Professor of Literature at Duke University

fact that the problem still exists.

People have long memories, even if some historians have tried to airbrush problems of injustice out of the history books. Black citizens in America will tell you the problem goes back 400 years to the abomination that was the savage cruelty of slavery, Irish people have not forgotten the injustices visited on them by 800 years of English rule, and the many Commonwealth citizens of the Windrush era who were wrongly detained, deported and denied legal rights will not readily forget the treatment meted out to them by British 'justice'. So institutional racism has been with us for a very long time and will persist for as long as there are those who are contemptuous of anyone who is 'different'- people they have been brought up to believe are their inferiors and not to be trusted. The present situation brings to mind the words of Daniel Berrigan S.J. referring to protests at the time of the Vietnam War:

"We were asking for a President who would obey the mandate that had given him office. We were asking for police forces that would eschew violence as their primary tactic. We were demanding that citizens accept the law of the land with regard to equal access to education and housing and jobs, for all, white or black.

Our hopes were modest. But in the rapid explosions of public fury since 1954, our hopes one by one were dashed. Law and Order were violated almost universally. They were violated first of all and most frequently by those who cried to us as a slogan of social salvation, "Law and order!" The citizenry was racist, the police were violent, the Congress was delinquent, the courts were conniving. "[54]

The fact that the killing of George Floyd sparked so many protests, not only in America but around the world, and the encouraging number of young people of all colours and creeds who have participated in those protests, gives one hope that perhaps this time the protests might prove a catalyst for a much needed change in social attitudes to people of other races and faiths. However, the recent booing of footballers by certain supporters for 'taking the knee' in support of the 'Black lives matter' campaign shows there is no room for complacency. There is still much to be done.

The unity and determination shown by people in the fight against the corona virus pandemic and the self-sacrifice of frontline workers, especially in the intensive care units of our hospitals, is another cause for optimism. After all who could fail to recognise the ultimate sacrifice paid by so many of our medical staff and care workers, or to recognise the fact that, among them, there has been an inordinate number of fatalities from our Black, Asian and Minority Ethnic communities.

Of course, there are still those determined to foment division with their tiresome and dangerous campaigns of hatred of people whom they consider to be inferior and it is sad to hear that some young black men and women today are still of the opinion that racism will never change or 'perhaps only in 200 years'. I have often heard the same sentiment expressed in relation to sectarianism in Scotland, but I have to believe that, with education, even those still fighting centuries old battles might eventually come to realise that the cancer of hatred of other races or religions is corrosive, not only to their own health and well-being but also to the

[54] Daniel Berrigan S.J. No Bars to Manhood, p42

safety and security of the society in which they live.

I am not totally naïve. You cannot live eighty years without experiencing the good and the bad that life throws up. I understand that many people see change as a threat to their way of life, even when change may be necessary to bring about improvement to that way of life. Any change which might promote harmony and coexistence among people from different countries, races or religions, for example, can only be beneficial to society as a whole. During our many conversations Luis and I frequently return to the mutual confidence and faith we have in our young people and their ability to confront the problems which our generation will bequeath to them. Personally, I have never subscribed to the jaundiced and cynical view that it is all very well for people to have ideals in their youth but that they will inevitably become disillusioned with age. I simply refuse to accept the premise that every young idealist will be prepared to abandon his or her principles in later years when, according to the cynics, the harsh realities of life will necessarily prove that the idealism of their youth was just that, and that they will come to realise that, *"Man is not made for utopian societies."*[55]

Personally, I am encouraged by the number of young people of all colours and creeds involved in the Black Lives Matter protests; the leading part our youth play in the climate change movement; the positive involvement of young voters in the U.S. elections and, in particular, their rejection of the divisive politics of the Trump administration; and, despite criticism of their occasional ill-advised social gatherings, the many youthful volunteers who participate in schemes to support vulnerable citizens during the covid-19

---

[55] Ernesto Sábato: Sobre Héroes y Tumbas, p104

pandemic. I am hopeful that the totally negative and destructive age-old *Us* and *Them* mentality which has reeked such havoc in communities around the world is at last being seriously challenged.

Change is organic and in terms of the progress necessary to overcome historic prejudices and injustices can be painfully slow. In order to speed up the process we could start by following the example of our young people. We have to recognise that nothing can be changed unless and until the problem of racism, bigotry and sectarianism is tackled. It would be all too easy to give in to despair at the ease with which people can be turned against one another; to despair at the cynicism of those who use ignorance and fear of the 'other' for their own ends; and to succumb to despair when faced with the cruel consequences visited on so many countless people as a result of such cynicism. Instead, let's face and embrace the strangers in our midst and concentrate on the positive contribution they make to our vibrant, multicultural society. Let's all do what we can to convince those enslaved by hatred that their lives would be so much richer if they could only learn to celebrate differences. As we have so often been reminded during the present pandemic, we are all in this together and like it or not we need each other. We would do well to take on board the words of Scotland's national bard:

> *Then let us pray that come it may,*
> *As come it will for a' that,*
> *That sense and worth, o'er a' the earth,*
> *May bear the gree, an' a' that.*
> *For a' that, an a' that,*
> *That man to man, the world o'er,*

Shall brothers be for a' that.[56]

A naïve hope perhaps, given the continuing attacks on minorities in many parts of the world. Of course, hope in itself is not enough. Every generation has to engage in the process of reconciliation between peoples if we are to make any progress in our efforts to persuade communities to avoid the type of divisions and distrust of democratic principles encouraged by Donald Trump's irresponsible, often irrational and outlandish comments. His repeated assertions about voter fraud and a stolen election win encouraged his most vociferous and dangerous supporters to violently storm the Capitol Building in Washington in January 2020 - an incursion which resulted in the death of five U.S. citizens. Unfortunately, as daily television reports have shown, his views have struck a chord with millions of Americans who have felt ignored for too long by the political establishment. As a result, the 2020 Presidential election has highlighted a country now riven by bitter divisions and recriminations. However, it would be short-sighted in the extreme if we thought that the problem of divisions between sections of a country was confined to the United States. We, in the so-called United Kingdom, have our own problems in that regard, as do most countries. It is the responsibility of all of us, wherever we live in the world, to strive to bring about more inclusive societies. Whatever the root causes of our particular allegiances and divisions – whether geographical or historical - it would serve all of us well to remember the words of John Hume the Northern Irish politician who dedicated his life to peace in his homeland: "*Our humanity*

---

[56] Robert Burns: For a' That and a' That

181

transcends our identity." Only when we accept the truth of that statement will we come to the realisation that:

"We and Them are shadows of each other. We are Them to Them as They are Them to Us."[57]

---

[57] R.D.Laing: The Politics of Experience, P83

Appendix A

Not even a small country like El Salvador was safe from the far-reaching tentacles of 'Operation Condor' and the Latin American military graduates of the U.S Army training centre, the 'School of the Americas.'

People of El Salvador
I sympathise with you.
I have read the reports
Of rape, killings and torture
In your country.

I believe these reports to be true.
For I have seen the corpses
Rotting in the streets of your cities
And your refugees wending their pitiful way
Into neighbouring states.

I have seen death on the steps
of San Salvador's cathedral
and learned with horror
of the fate of your champion,
Romero - ¡Qué en paz descanse!

I sympathise with you
People of El Salvador.
I recognise that you wish to be treated with dignity.
I accept that your children ought not to be deprived
Of food, clothing, shelter, education and adequate
Medical care.

But people of El Salvador
My government and the media in my country
Tell me that you are oppressed by an unacceptable
    'ism'
And so, while the misery of your life is regrettable,
Those who perpetuate that misery
Must be maintained in power
Lest the benefits of our free, civilised
And Christian way of life
Be lost to you forever.

People of El Salvador
I weep for you.....
And for my silence and my shame.

Airdrie, April 1980

Appendix B

In 1977 as part of preparations for participation in the 1978 World Cup in Argentina, Scotland's National football team played a match against Chile in the National Stadium in Santiago de Chile, despite the torture and executions which took place there after the military coup. SFA officials obviously felt that this was not sufficient reason to forego the opportunity to play the game nor indeed to meet a three-man delegation of ex-prisoners of the military Junta. This despite the fact that Russia forfeited the chance of qualifying for a place in the World Cup by refusing to take part in a play-off against Chile.

Blood on the Grass

September the eleventh in Nineteen seventy-three
Scores of people perished in a vile machine-gun spree
Santiago stadium became a place to kill
But a Scottish football team will grace it with their skill
And there's blood upon the grass
And there's blood upon the grass

Will you go there Alan Rough, will you go there Tom Forsyth
Where so many folk met early the Grim Reaper with his Scythe
These people weren't terrorists they weren't Party hacks,
But some were maybe goalkeepers and some were centre backs
And there's blood upon the grass
And there's blood upon the grass

Victor Jara played guitar as he was led into the ground
Then they broke all of his fingers so his strings no more
could sound
Still he kept on singing songs of freedom songs of
peace
And though they gunned him down his message doesn't
cease
And there's blood upon the grass
And there's blood upon the grass

Will you go there Archie Gemmill, will you go there
Andy Gray
Will it trouble you to hear the voice of Victor Jara say
Somos cinco mil, we are five thousand in this place
And Scottish football helps to hide the Junta's dark
disgrace
And there's blood upon the grass
And there's blood upon the grass

Do you stand upon the terracing at Ibrox or Parkhead?
Do you cheer the Saints in black and white, the Dons
in flaming red?
All those who died in Chile were people of your kind
Let's tell the football bosses that it's time they changed
their mind
Before there's blood upon their hands.

(Song by Adam McNaughton)

Bibliography

Media Control: Noam Chomsky, (Seven Stories Press)

Chavs: Owen Jones, (Verso Books)

One Dimensional Man: Herbert Marcuse, (Sphere Books Ltd)

No Bars to Manhood: Daniel Berrigan S.J. (Bantam Books)

The Politics of Experience and The Bird of Paradise: R.D.Laing, (Penguin Books)

The Shock Doctrine: Naomi Klein, (Penguin Books)

El Mercado y la Globalización: José Luis Sampedro, (Ediciones Destino)

Trials of the State: Jonathan Sumption, (Profile Books)

21 Lessons for the 21st Century: Yuval Noah Harari, (Vintage, Penguin Random House)

El Enemigo del Pueblo: Jim Acosta, (Harper Collins Ibérico)

La Planète des Singes: Pierre Boulle, Editions G.P. Paris)

Talking to my Daughter: Yanis Varoufakis, (Vintage)

How Democracies Die: Steven Levitsky & Daniel Ziblatt, (Penguin Books)

12 Rules for Life: Jordan B Peterson, (Penguin Books)

The Future of Work: Robots, AI and Automation: Darrell M West, (Brooking Institution Press)

Franco: Soldier, Commander, Dictator: Geoffrey Jenson, (Potomac Books)

Days of Hope: André Malraux, (Penguin)

The Spanish Holocaust: Paul Preston, (Harper Press)

In Hiding-The Life of Manuel Cortes: Ronald Fraser, (Penguin)

La Rebelión de las Masas: José Ortega y Gasset (Revista de Occidente, Madrid)

Barça: Jimmy Burns, (Bloomsburg Publishing)

Homage to Catalonia: George Orwell, (Secker and Warburg)

Yo Augusto: Ernesto Ekaizer, (Aguilar)

Church and Colonialism: Helder Camara, (Sheed and Ward)

Of Love and Shadows: Isabel Allende, (Black Swan)

Estadio de Chile, 1973: Mauricio Brum (Unijui)

La question de Kosovo: Ibrahim Rugova, (Fayard)

The New Threat from Islamic Militancy: Jason Burke, (Vintage)

The Ragged Trousered Philanthropists: Robert Tressell, (Granada)

Prisoners of Geography: Tim Marshall, (Elliott and Thompson Ltd)

Acknowledgements

This book would never have been completed without the support of my wife who tolerated the countless hours I spent in my study constantly re-drafting what I had written. I'm sure she would have preferred me to have spent less time on the laptop and more on family matters.

Particular thanks must go to my good friend Luis Ignacio Ramallo Massanet whose encouragement and contributions were invaluable. We spent many hours recording our experiences of particular historical events which highlighted the damaging effect of the failure to recognise and respect differences between peoples. During these discussions our thoughts would invariably turn to education as the best way to encourage mutual understanding, healing, and respect.

I should also like to include my appreciation of the input of Don Manuel Parra Martinez and his charming wife Doña Hermanna Wörm who took the time to sit down with a relative stranger in order to fill in some details of their early years together in Spain. Their kindness was matched by that shown to my family by all staff members of their restaurant, the Cala Canta where my wife and I were always warmly received on our regular visits.

Grateful thanks must also go to the many authors listed in the bibliography. Their contribution and influence can be readily seen throughout this work. Nor can I fail to recognise the part played in my journey through life by the countless unnamed individuals I have encountered from childhood to my eightieth year. Each and every one has taught me something invaluable about life, though I may not have recognised it at the time. I am who I am because of the influence they have had on me.

A special mention and grateful thanks to my nephew, Paul McGinlay, who gave up much of his valuable time to read over the final draft and highlight a few discrepancies – it is amazing how many details one misses no matter how many times a work is revisited.

Special thanks are also due to my good friend Tony Beekman for his many helpful suggestions and to my son Edward, and grand-daughter Megan, without whom the intricacies of the laptop would have remained a total mystery. I'm sure they must have wondered whether I would ever master even the basics of 'Word.'

Illustrations

Ramallo Massamet

The exploitation of hatred, fear and suspicion of the *'other,'* whether due to political, religious or racial differences, has been a constant throughout human history. Down through the ages unscrupulous kings, tyrants, politicians and populists have played on the ignorance of people in order to maintain themselves in power, with little regard to the often inevitable bloody consequences. This account of the recollections of two old friends is written in the hope that it might persuade some readers of the futility and indeed the absurdity of an *'Us and Them'* mentality. Peaceful co-existence requires all of us to recognise that:

"Difference is of the essence of humanity. Difference is an accident of birth and it should therefore never be the source of hatred or conflict. The answer to difference is to respect it. Therein lies a most fundamental principle of peace – respect for diversity."

John Hume

Lightning Source UK Ltd.
Milton Keynes UK
UKHW012050250821
389453UK00001B/93